Catalogue of Bee Books collected and offered for sale

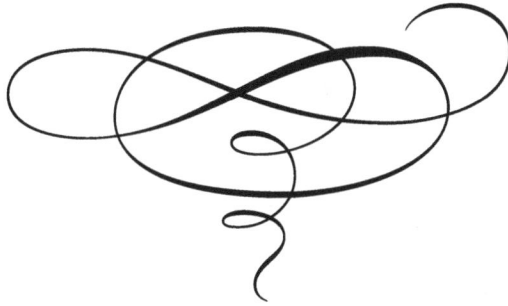

by
Geoffrey Lawes
of
Billingshurst, West Sussex

October, 2009

with a foreword by Michael Freedman

Northern Bee Books

Ephemeral engraving of 1866 "The British Workman".

"This good man can tell much about the bees – their way of
life, their industry, their skill, and their uses in God's world.
He has kept bees for a long time…. and has read trustworthy
books about them."

Descriptive Catalogue of a Library of Bee Books collected and offered for sale

© Geoffrey Lawes

October 2009

ISBN 978-1-904846-43-7

Published by Northern Bee Books, 2009
Scout Bottom Farm
Mytholmroyd
Hebden Bridge HX7 5JS (UK

Foreword to catalogue

When I was first introduced to the wonders of bee-keeping as a rookie, collecting a swarm and learning the hard way, from ones mistakes, my mentor and tutor, Ernie Longworth, explained to me that bee-keeping means many different things to those who indulge in the craft.

To some it provides honey, wax and other bee products, while to others, there is the scientific aspect, dealing with pheromones and entomology. Many find art and beauty in the amazing structures built by bees, likening them to architects and builders of cities. Yet others delve into the social structures of a society which has prospered over many millions of years, well before man's civilisation. Some obtain medical knowledge and remedies from propolis and venom. Then there are those who wish to advance the craft and deepen the mutual benefit of man and bee. The importance in economics of bee-keeping has been apparent throughout the ages.

So too, all these and many more aspects are reflected in the world of bee books and anyone with that collector's gene will soon be hooked by the bug.

There is a long thread of knowledge and insight which has passed through many generations and those with the gift to record these in a literary fashion have passed a baton from one to the other.

In this way great works have been written, some in art, like the ideas expressed in the works of Virgil, embodying myth and legend, while others brought to bear great breakthroughs in knowledge, beginning with Charles Butler, in 1609, with his Feminine Monarchie. A polymath, Butler had the ability to tie in his observations with the world of music and science and his book was widely sought after and was translated into Latin and then retranslated back into English in 1704 by "W.S.". The artistry of the frontis is truly inspirational and to own a copy of this and realise how 400 years ago the work served to enlighten our bee-keeping forerunners, can only give a spiritual feeling of being one of a band of like-minded individuals who thirst to be part of and involved with an amazingly great interest and practice.

Many of the authors refer to ideas put forward by both past masters and contemporary bee-keepers, creating a chain of thought and knowledge down the centuries to the present day. We collectors can identify and gain strength in our purpose from progress in understanding.

In 1744, the Reverend John Thorley produced Melisselogia or The female monarchy and as well as admiring the superior social order of the hive, performed scientific observations by temporarily anesthetising the bees with puffball smoke. This is beautifully illustrated in his book.

Thomas Wildman's Treatise, came from a great bee man, who had fully mastered the art and practice of bee-keeping. He offered his services to look after apiaries for a fee to subscribers within three miles of London. His nephew, Daniel harnessed the commercial potential from his warehouse in the Holborn.

In 1795, James Bonner, tells of how he raised his family from the sale of produce of the apiary and how all could benefit in this way and overcome poverty. Up to this time 151 books are listed in the British Bee Books bibliography, comprising a precious repository of fact and some fiction.

The output of authors in the 19th century produced 250 listed works and with the advances in printing, papermaking and retailing, these books and the instruction and enlightenment they provided reached a far wider readership.

Great men such as Francis Huber and Thomas Nutt wrote about humanity towards bees. The Rules of the British Apiarian Society were published and William Cobbett exhorted cottagers to keep bees to improve their economic lot.

Cooks and housekeepers such as Mary Eaton whose work of 1842 extolled the virtues of the apiary and its products in everyday household life, exemplified this age.

Humble gardeners such as Matthew Pile of Gateshead in 1838 and John Wighton, gardener to Lord Stafford in 1842, showed how writing books was not just the product of the highly educated and reached the realms of the working man.

In the eighteenth century books were often presold and the subscriber lists appear in them. Some of these signed their copies and a further tangible link with the past is evident. Then books and libraries were the exclusive domain of the gentry. In the 19th century, books were produced in thousands and sold for as little as a penny or more often for 6 pence or a shilling.

Alfred Neighbour's book The Apiary, published 1865, beautifully illustrates his Commercial Apiary in Hampstead Lane in the third edition which appeared in 1878.

Many revered and highly knowledgeable bee-keepers were able now to record their experiences and the art of bee-keeping with skeps was definitively covered by Pettigrew in 1870 with his Handy Book of Bees.

Building on this, the 20th century disseminated a veritable explosion of books, with a further 412 listed in BBB up to 1977. Great figures emerged such as William Herrod-Hempsall who describes how he and his brother passaged from barefoot poor Nottingham boys, to walking with King George Vth at the 1929 Wembley exhibition. They had started by helping bee-keepers obtain their wax and honey by driving the bees instead of killing them and in return, keeping the bees they had saved from suffocation. They put their advancement in life down to the bees.

Since 1977, many hundreds of books have emerged, some instructive in the craft, some for children as an insight into nature and others covering every detail of ecology, leading on to the challenges of the 21st century, facing and dealing with the effects of the Varoa mite and Colony Collapse Disorder.

All of this and much more has been embraced by Geoff Lawes, a bee book collector of great stature and generosity, by producing his painstaking work of cataloguing his extensive and diverse collection, varying from the old masters, to present day. In his 1991 work, The Bee Book Book, Geoffrey has given us an insight into amassing and caring for a collection and how to record and display a specialist subject library.

It is fitting that his catalogue should be sought after and valued among the exceptional listings of bee books which we have and love.

Michael Freedman, 2009

Bee Book Collections *Reviewed by Martin Tovey*

'But are there not more than enough bee books?'
Karl von Frisch and my wife.

I have been asked to comment on some of the more notable collections of bee books over the years. As an avid collector of bee books I leapt at the opportunity to own a bee book business when Tony Davies offered me 'Honeyfield Books' some twenty- five years ago. This was later sold to Karl Showler, who renamed it B & K Books, and latterly sold to C.Arden books in Hay-on Wye.

Most great bee book collections were started by one man and then bought or inherited by another bibliophile and here lies some of the more interesting histories of provenance of great collections.

The Charles C. Miller Memorial Library (over 5000 titles) at the University of Wisconsin has an intriguing background involving Tegetmeier, Neighbour and Lt.-Col.Walker. William Bernhardt Tegetmeier (1816-1912) was educated at University College and became a founder member of the Royal Entomological Society. He was a pigeon fancier, who introduced long distance pigeon racing into Britain, as well as writing an established standard book on Poultry and Pheasants. He wrote in 'The Field' until he was over ninety and was their Natural History Editor for over fifty years. He became interested in bees in the 1850s and corresponded with Charles Darwin. Darwin mentions Tegetmeier's studies on the formation of cells in the comb in his books on 'Origin of Species' and on poultry in 'Animals and Plants under Domestication'. Tegetmeier wrote only one book 'Bees, Hives and Honey' but contributed to entries in 'Encyclopaedia Britannica' and references to his work appear in Thomas Cowan's 'The Honey Bee'. Tegetmeier's bee book collection was purchased by Alfred Neighbour (1825-1890), son of George Neighbour, who was a great 19th century bee appliance manufacturer. The firm were fortunate to be agents for Thomas Nutt and Alfred often accompanied Nutt on visits to the firm's customers. The Neighbours managed a public apiary at the Zoological Gardens in Regents Park, which is illustrated, both interior and exterior, at the back of his book 'The Apiary'. Their stand at the International Exhibition of 1862 is also shown in 'The Apiary' where Neighbour's Unicomb Observatory hive was stocked with Ligurian (Italian) bees first introduced to Britain by T.W.Woodbury in 1859. When Neighbour died in 1890 a large proportion of his collection went to form the nucleus of Lt.-Col.Walker's bee book collection. Lt.-Col. Herbert John Oucherlony Walker (1843-1934) first became interested in beekeeping through reading a copy of Cheshire's book, 'Bees and Beekeeping' in 1886. Lt-Col.Walker is gratefully acknowledged to have spent two weeks at the offices of the British Bee Journal (BBJ) in the Strand re-cataloguing the 1882 catalogue and making a Card Index of the library of the British Beekeeping Association (BBKA) in 1912. The 'Catalogue of Bee Books collected and offered by Lt.-Col.Walker' was published in 1929 and was purchased by the Miller Memorial Library in Wisconsin, USA.

Harrison Ashforth says that the reason the Walker collection was not purchased by the BBKA was that they had just completed their purchase of the 1800 volume collection of their late President and founder member, Dr. Thomas William Cowan (1840-1926). Dr.Cowan was the first chairman of the BBKA, an office he held continually for 48 years, in addition to being proprietor and editor of BBJ from 1885. Cowan is certainly counted as one of the greats in British Beekeeping. His 'British Beekeeping Guide Book', first published in 1881, ran until its twenty-fourth edition in 1924 with over 100,000 copies. Dr.Cowans' death was attributed to falling off some steps whilst reaching for a book from his collection. Dr.Cowan's collection was purchased by the Ministry of Agriculture, Fisheries and Food for £260 and housed at Whitehall, but is now at Sand Hutton, York.

One of the world's greatest collection of apicultural literature is housed at the Albert. R. Mann Library at Cornell University in Ithaca, NY, USA. This was started by Prof. Everett Franklin Phillips in 1925, who persuaded 223 people from twenty-nine states and twenty-six foreign countries to donate thousands of books and pamphlets. He also initiated an endowment by persuading hundreds of New York beekeepers to set aside one of their hives for the Library until a $50 threshold had been donated. It is thought that some of the Rev. Lorenzo Lorraine Langstroth's notable collection ended up in the Cornell Library. Langstroth (1810-1895) is known as the Father of American Beekeeping. Florence Naile, his biographer, refers to American Bee Journal Nov 28 1895 vol xxxv, page 765 for the list. Langstroth's daughter, Mrs.H.C.Cowan, who married T.W.Cowan's son, sought for a college to buy the collection as a lot of about 100 books but they were sold to a dealer and dispersed, though some fifty volumes found their way to Cornell. Some rare beekeeping works are now on-line including the first twenty years of the 'American Bee Journal' 1861-1884.

Scotland's greatest collection is the result of another avid bibliophile, John William Moir (1851-1940). Moir started beekeeping during his thirteen years in Africa because he required better pollination of his crops but on returning to Scotland in 1890 continued beekeeping as a hobby. In 1912 he became one of the original founders of the Scottish Beekeeping Association (SBA) and started seriously to collect bee books. By 1916 he owned 167 volumes and decided to bequeath the books to the Scottish Beekeepers' Association and act as Hon. Librarian and continue to house the collection at his home.

In 1933 a catalogue was issued showing 1270 items but with failing health the library was transferred to the Edinburgh Public Library in 1939 with some 1799 books and pamphlets. Since 2002 the rare books are now kept at the National Library of Scotland and the balance are held at the Fountainbridge Library, Edinburgh.

William Charles Cotton (1813-1879), a student of Christ Church, Oxford lists about 125 valuable books in his work 'My Bee Book'. His own collection ran to over 200 rare works and he acknowledges titles from collections of a Mr.Dawson of Botesdale in Suffolk, Mr.J.H.Payne, author of 'The Apiarian's Guide' and John Milton who wrote 'The Practical Beekeeper'1843. In this latter book notes left by Cotton were put to unauthorised use, and a row ensued when Cotton returned from New Zealand. His collection was bequeathed to his parish of Frodsham, Cheshire, which retains ownership but was deposited in the library of the Ministry of Agriculture, Fisheries and Food in 1932 and transferred to the University of Reading in 1987. The University also holds some thirty pre 1851 works owned by H.Malcolm Fraser as well as his own collection of papers.

The largest collection of apicultural literature in Britain started relatively recently in 1949 with the formation of the Bee Research Association (BRA), which came about as a result of the actions of the scientists on the Research Committee of the British Beekeepers Association. BRA started in March 1949 and by December had over 1000 publications. The largest initial part came from the Apis Club but in 1964, The Morland Bequest greatly enriched the collection. By 1973 following the W.Essinger Bequest of the previous year there were nearly 29,000 publications. Many famous names helped in creating the collection including J.Pryce Jones, Bro.Adam, Miss A.D.Betts, Miss M.D.Bindley, E.G. and M.G.Burtt, Eva Crane, H.A. Dade, A.G. Eames, Dr.H.M. Fraser, Miss Dorothy Hodges, Miss Dorothy Galton, C.C. Tonsley and Mrs.W. Wedmore (E.B. Wedmore's widow). Graham Burtt came across a copy of Langstroth's book 'The Hive and the Honeybee' that Langstroth presented to T.W. Woodbury of Exeter, the beemaster who introduced the movable frame hive into Britain. Burtt gave this book to IBRA. The pre 1900 books still remain with IBRA at Cardiff (some 600 volumes) but the bulk of the collection of post 1900 books and pamphlets representing fifteen tons of material went as the Eva Crane Memorial Library to the National Library of Wales, Aberystwyth. An illustration of the professional care of National libraries is that on receipt of this consignment, it was all quarantined, and then every book was placed in a partial vacuum sink whilst each page was cleaned of any spores.

A.L.Gregg in 'The Philosophy and Practice of Beekeeping' urges Associations to keep lending libraries of bee books and many County and branch Associations maintain good depositories available to their members.

A county Association Library, which I know due to serving as an official, is that of Hampshire. It is the oldest with a sad history, and had its first catalogue printed in the Hants and Isle of Wight Beekeepers' Association (HBA) annual report of 1884, and lists some forty-one treasured works, which by 1907 had risen to eighty-one. In 1930 the council bought a copy of all of Mace's books and distributed 100 copies of his 'Beekeepers Manual' to the members. H.P.Young allowed his books to be added to the library in 1939 which continued until after his death in 1961 after forty years service to HBA. The library was renamed the H.P. Young Memorial Library and then contained 270 different titles, when in 1966 disaster struck. The Bee Department at the college of Agriculture, Sparsholt was destroyed by fire and many of the priceless books lost- fortunately a number were out on loan. After an appeal for more books by Capt.Tredwell the library was up to 166 titles by 1968. 'Hogs at the Honeypot' by Frank Vernon lists over 600 separate titles and 'British Bee Books' bibliography lists only Hampshire as a county association with an important collection of bee books. I do know that as a result of a bequest in 2005 by Sid Pullinger the library benefited from even more titles. At national level the British Beekeepers Association has recently had two generous bequests. Marjorie Knights left George Knights' contemporary collection of some three hundred titles to the BBKA- as well as a large financial sum and the granddaughter of Herbert Mace left a comprehensive collection of all his books and pamphlets including his 1929 criticism of the BBKA.

British Bee Book Bibliography lists 11 major British library collections and three in the USA together with 10 other important collections worldwide and Johannson lists another three in the States in his book 'Apicultural literature published in Canada and the United States'. For a Russian perspective on beekeeping literature, the most accessible bibliography is that of Naum Ioyrish who devotes 27 pages of 'Bees and People' to the task.

Lastly there are the individuals, bee book dealers and publishers. Jeremy Burbidge of Northern Bee Books was lucky enough to obtain the Gregg collection as well as a vast quantity of books from David Bone. Karl Showler has amassed a sizeable number from trading as B&K Books and for myself I was most fortunate to be offered the book collection of my mentor, Frank Vernon, by Mary his widow, as well as many from Tom Shutte and Harrison Ashforth. Geoff Lawes lists a number of titles from the Sussex author Rev. Tickner Edwardes' collection as well as a number owned by A.M.Sturges. I know of a number of other large private collections in the UK but without their permission to publish feel reluctant to quote their names. I wish you all Happy and Successful collecting.

Martin Tovey

2009

Geoffrey Lawes – Collector and Vendor

Geoff Lawes was born in 1930 at Castle Acre, West Norfolk. He was first conscious of bees and hives at the age of 5 in the garden of Mrs Lees, Headmistress, at Henham School in Suffolk. After wartime schooling, national service, a year of farm work and a spell as a junior clerk to the Royal Norfolk Show, he trained as a teacher at Goldsmiths College, Univ of London and graduated again with Hons in English at Birkbeck College in 1958. He taught in Lewisham until 1974 at Catford and Sedgehill Schools. In 1965, he spent a year as an exchange teacher in Fargo, N. Dakota and subsequently became Head of Roger Manwood School, Brockley. He then left London for West Sussex to return to his rural roots as Headmaster of The Weald School, a mixed comprehensive school for 1500 11 to 18 year olds. There he was drawn into beekeeping by Alan Dugdale, Head of Rural Studies, and developed that interest through practice, pupil involvement, macro-photography, microscopy and not least by collecting books on the subject. The school Bee Club formed a small part of the school's vision of a local liberal education, and enjoyed success in classes at the National Honey Show.

Geoff collected this largely British library of books on bees and beekeeping over a period of 35 years as a diversion, together with maintaining his own apiaries. The steady pursuit of items from boot sales, second-hand bookshops, national dealers and auction houses has caused the collection to mount to over 1100 volumes with about 550 different titles.

In the pre-computer, video and DVD era of the 70s and 80s he undertook lecturing on beekeeping, running woodworking evening classes for hive building, making numerous slide-tape instructional programmes for the

BBKA library for loan to bee clubs and acting as photographic judge for the National Honey Show.

In 1991, encouraged by Jeremy Burbidge of Northern Bee Books, he prepared 'The Bee Book Book' which offered information and advice on the making and maintenance of a bee book collection. This was further informed by editorial and illustrative work on Irmgard Diemer's book 'Bees and Beekeeping' and other publications and contributions to Wisborough Green BKA, West Sussex, where he learned a great deal from many wise and experienced practitioners such as Roger Patterson, Jack Holt and George Wakeford. His other published writings are on educational matters, including, in 2007, the 50 year History of the Weald School.

In retirement, Geoff spent 10 years as a County and District Councillor but now enjoys bees, golf, and the comforts and adventures of his family, house and garden, and reading the good books he had neglected in his youth.

INTRODUCTION

Descriptive Catalogue

Following the precedent of the catalogue of bee books offered for sale by Lt.Col. H.J.O. Walker in 1929 the individual items are priced separately, though the Collection is for sale as a whole or in parts. Appropriate agreed discounts are available in relation to the number and value of the volumes sought by the purchaser. The prices stated are based on those customary in the retail trade assessed by reference to current dealers' lists and auction prices and are quoted in Pounds Sterling, which, by computation, would value the Library at about £45,000. Col Walker's list was sold for 3/6d, roughly equivalent to £8 today He valued his magnificent collection at only £347. It was wisely acquired by the University of Wisconsin as part of the Miller Library. Like 1929, the year 2009 AD is one of international recession when the pound is at a low exchange rate with both the Euro and the Dollar and subject to frequent variations. In consequence potential purchasers must needs make their own necessary conversions.

Straitened economic conditions may prove to have a depressive effect on the currency value of the books. However the vendor is conscious that rare and collectable old books have their own honest intrinsic value. Subject to protection from fire, flood, the fickleness of fashion and other fiascos their value is unlikely to diminish with the passage of years or suffer from the accidents and uncertainties of most other tangible assets and currencies. Indeed the passing of 80 years since Col. Walker issued his catalogue will have appreciated the value of the ever-shrinking pool of worthy artefacts available to those who enjoy the scholarship, literary and artistic qualities and experience captured within their covers.

THE PRESENTATION OF THE CATALOGUE

The catalogue is presented in one continuous alphabetical sequence, based on the authors' names. To assist users whose interest lies in particular areas or eras, each numerical reference has an entry after the price on the bottom line which places the book in one of eight categories as follows:

1. ANTiquarian - all books to 1850
2. OLD - 1851 to 1918
3. 20th Century 1919 to 1976
4. MODern - 1977 to date
5. USA - Published in N.America
6. BAB - Books about Books
7. FOReign - in languages other than English
8. MISCellaneous - Insects,techniques and related topics

Thus to scan the list for any particular category, one can see what is available by skimming through the pages picking out the identifying symbol.

Each book carries a Lot or Reference No. There are many duplicated titles, repeated where edition, condition, price or other factors differentiate a volume from the initial entry. However, to avoid tedious repetition, where two or more copies are available of a title these are grouped as one lot and the number available stated. The price is then for any one copy unless otherwise indicated.

Each entry also carries the Author's identity, the title, date of first publication, edition where known and date of issue. Then follows a brief statement about the condition of the book It can be assumed for the sake of brevity that all the books are 'good' or 'very good' where nothing else is stated. In the event of a buyer being dissatisfied with the state of a purchase, the price will be refunded on the return of the volume in the condition when received.

Finally comments are offered on each title in the belief that the making of this catalogue, of a wide range of beekeeping books, offers a rare opportunity to enhance its informative value. A short critique is given of the individual subject matter and the status of the person who wrote the book. "Bee Books" embrace many genres - instruction books, manuals, anatomical studies, poems, artistic and literary vehicles, childrens' diversions and moral tracts to name but a few. Accordingly information is proffered on the life and reputations of authors, their significant or interesting contributions to the craft and beekeeping literature, and the style and nature of the work. Extracts from reviews by prominent and reliable critics are commonly employed and are acknowledged with thanks.

KEY TO ENTRIES

IBRA or US no. 1st Pub Yr Edition Yr Edition Condition and number of copies

21 **Andrewes, Sir C** *The Lives of Bees & Wasps*

543 1969 - 1st dw 16 plates. Bibliography.Ex-lib.

Comments — Demonstrates the stages of evolution from solitary to fully social in many guide to Latin names.

Title — 30 - 20thC -

Author

Reference no. — **22** **Andrews, S W** *All About Mead*

544 1971 - 1st (2 copies)

Mills and Boon

8 2 20thC

Cost Copies Category

1   A.L.O.E   *Wings and Stings*

284 J574   1855   1872   1879   6th   . . Nicely bound with a decorative cover.A Night School Prize 1881

A Lady of England Charlotte Maria Tucker A tale for the young. Many excellent drawings of Victorian children.

20   -   OLD

2   Abbott, C P *Queen Breeding for Amateurs*

532   1947   1947   1st   Signed inscription to Mr.Rouse. H/b dw

Charles Pryce Abbott MBE [1893-1973] Third generation of heirs to CN Abbott who absorbed the Neighbour business in 1895. CNA launched The British Bee Journal in 1872 and the BBKA in 1874, ran a "School of Apiculture" and fathered The Abbott Standard Hive. CPA made films on beekeeping with Colin Butler,including one on artificial insemination and was Treasurer of Bee Diseases Insurance Ltd. A Bee Craft book.

12   - 20^{th}C

---

3   Abbott, C P *Another*

532   1947   1947   1st   Limp copy-

8   - 20^{th}C

---

4   Abbott, C P *Another*

532   1947   1951   3   1st of new & revised (3 copies)

10   3 20^{th}C

---

5   Abbott , May   *Me & the Bee*

533   1965   -   1st   -

:the Battles of a Bumbling Beekeeper An amusing self-deprecating beginner's story.

20   - 20^{th}C

---

6   Abushady   *The Bee Kingdom. Volume X No.1*

-        1939   -   1st   Spine taped.

Root Memorial booklet

20   - 20^{th}C

7   Acton & Duncan *Making Mead*

534   1965   1972   9th imp   .(2 copies)

a complete guide...sweet and dry mead,melomel,hippocras,pyment and cyser.Amateur Winemaker

8   2 20^{th}C

---

8   Acton & Duncan *Another*

534   1965   1985   16th imp -   -

8   - 20^{th}C

Geoffrey Lawes

9   Adam, Brother OBE   *Beekeeping at Buckfast Abbey*
535   1971   1977   -   Reprint. Signed by author
with a section on meadmaking. Bro. Adam was born 1898 as Karl Kerle. Novice at Buckfast 1914 where he kept the bees for 70 years
20   -   20thC

10   Adam, Brother OBE   *Another*
535   1971   1980   -   Reprint. Limp   -
8   -   20thC

11   Adam, Brother OBE   *In Search of the Best Strains of Bees*
-    1966   1974   -   Signed. Paperback
"These travels have almost the sublimity and dedication of St Paul's missionary journeys" (Ron Brown)
15   -   20thC

12   Adam, Brother OBE   *Another*
-    1966   1974   -   h/b Northern Bee Books Near mint   -
15   -   20thC

13   Adam, Brother OBE   *Another*
-    1966   1974   -   pb   -
10   -   20thC

14   Aebi A and O   *Mastering the Art of Beekeeping*
-    1975   1982   1st UK   pb
Volume 1. Father and son write a friendly style book, telling how bees give them a living and how they broke the world record for wildflower honey from a single hive.
15   -   MOD

15   Alamanni, Luigi   *La Coltivazione de...*
-    1546   1718   -   Italian A large handsome tome
Luigi Alamanni & le Api di Giovanni Rucellai (of Florence). "An Italian poet and statesman, 1495-1556, was distinguished for the purity and excellence of his style. La Colt. Is in imitation of Virgil's Georgics. Rucellai (1449-1525) wrote 'Le Api' in imitation of the 4th Georgic. (Notes by Titi thereon) "This is a highly esteemed edition and has long been very scarce" (Walker) Has a magnificent frontispiece of Alamanni, also 4 handwritten notes with bee translation and comments.
300   -   FOR

16   Alfold, Dr DV   *The Life of the Bumblebee*
-    1978   -   1st   -   Nicely illustrated for the general reader. 25 UK species described.
15   -   MOD

17   Alfold,Dr DV   *Bumblebees*
540   1975   -   1st   -
56 plates,27 maps and a bibliography.The major authoritative work. 'Absorbing reading by an expert entomologist'(The Field).
45   -   MOD

18   Allen, Paul Marshall   *The Art of Beekeeping*
-        1975   -   1st   32 page booklet
Tasks for the beekeeper throughout the year.
8   -   USA

19   Alphandery, Raoul   *Un ruchet nait (40 lessons)*
-        1943   1946?   -   French.
French .Magnificent pictures. Ran to 5 editions with 50,000 sold. Father Edmond and his son, the French equivalents of Herrod-Hempsall,his close friend. Knight of the Legion of Honour. Edited 'La Gazette Apicole' for 40 years. Ron Brown recommends it for home study.
35   -   FOR

20   Anderson, Dr J   *Bees, Honey & Beekeeping*
542   1938   -   1st   Scottish Beekeepers' Association.
9 articles,mainly by Dr. Anderson. 2 plates
15   -   20thC

21   Andrewes, Sir C   *The Lives of Bees & Wasps*
543   1969   -   1st   dw 16 plates. Bibliography.Ex-lib.
Demonstrates the stages of evolution from solitary to fully social in many kinds of bees and wasps.Pronuncation guide to Latin names.
30   -   20thC

22   Andrews, S W   *All About Mead*
544   1971   -   1st   (2 copies)
Mills and Boon
8   2   20thC

23   Apimondia *I F B A 27th Congress*
-        1979   -   -   -
Collections of papers by international experts on a multiplicity of specialist topics.
12   -   MISC

24   Apimondia *I F B A 23rd Congress*
-        1971   -   -   -   -
12   -   MISC

25 Apimondia *I F B A 20th Congress*
- 1965 - - -
Jubilee Congress
12 - MISC

---

26 Armitt, J H *Beekeeping for Recreation & Profit*
546 1952 - 1st dw signed :
relating craftsmanship to the bee colony's natural development and instinctive behaviour. Advocates "nature's way" and "simple practice"
15 - 20thC

---

27 Armitt, J H *Another*
546 1952 - 1st (3 copies-2 with dw) -
12 3 20thC

---

28 Ash, E C *Ants, Bees & Wasps*
509 1924 - 1st Rare. Dedication by author to friend:
their Lives, Comedies and Tragedies. Nature Lovers Lib. Vol 23. Over140 text drawings giving colour and markings.
40 - 20thC

---

29 Atkinson, John *Beekeeping Technical Notes*
- 1983 - 1st pb typescript rare
Large format and duplicated. Written to assist Foul Brood Officers in dealing with bee diseases by the Ministry Beekeeping Adviser. Touches on Varroa. He was a commercial beekeeper, WW2 pilot and County Beekeeping Instructor. Master of artificial insemination and bee-breeding, beekeeping history and other quirky pursuits. Died 2008. "An iconoclast, with a slightly boyish sense of humour" (Pam Gregory)
20 - MOD

---

30 Bacon, Francis *Sylva Sylvarum*
23 1627 1676 10th Front cover and frontispiece plate of Bacon detached.
or a natural history in ten centuries. Includes 'Novum Organum'. 17th century polymath. Alleged by some to be author of Shakespeare's works, who 'took all knowledge to be his province' i.e. he knew everything there was to know. Published after the author's death by W Rawley D.D. Printed for T Lee at the sign of the Turk's Head, Fleet Street. 'The wisest, brightest, meanest of mankind' (Pope).
200 - ANT

---

31 Bagster, Samuel *The Management of Bees*
222 1834 - 1st Picture of three castes opposite title page missing.
:with a description of the Ladies Safety Hive, a complicated appliance. He was, like Nutt, an advocate of good hive ventilation. 40 wood engravings.
190 - ANT -

---

32 Bagster, Samuel *Another*
222 1834 1838 2nd Cover detatched. Very clean frontispiece of the British black bee.
Pub Saunders and Otley

100   -   ANT

---

33   Bagster, Samuel   *Another*

222   1834   1852   3rd   Saunders and Otley. Good frontispiece.

Saunders and Otley

130   -   ANT

---

34   Bailey, Dr L   *Infectious Diseases of the Honeybee*

548   1963   -   1st   -

Land Books. 8 plates Illustrated by JP Spradbury. An authoritative work on pathogens, diagnosis and control by a Rothamsted expert.

20   -   20thC

---

35   Bailey, Nat   *Dictionarium Rusticum, Urbanicum et Botanicum*

71   1704   1717   2nd   Rev by Nicholson and others   Signed Leverson-Gower

Recommends beer for stings plus a net and gloves. Otherwise various herbs or 'a live coal as near and as long as you can endure it'. 16 bee entries mostly derived from Worlidge and Hartlib. Follows Virgil too - bees generated from an ox carcass. A comprehensive resource in its time.

200   -   ANT

---

36   Baker, C T G   *Understanding the Honeybee*

549   1948   1974   -   Reprint. Shortened booklet   :

Anthroposophical Agricultural Foundation .Notes on the organic nature of the bee colony.

5   -   20thC

---

37   Barrett, P   *Australian Beekeeping Bibliography*

-    1997   1997   1st   Limp copy

Covers 1875-1995 38pps

15   -   BAB

---

38   Bazin, Gilles   *The Natural History of Bees*

96   1744   -   1st   -

Probably translated from the French of Reaumur by P. Vailant. Pub. J.P. Knapton (Ludgate Street) and Vailant (Strand). The Vailants were émigré booksellers at the time of the Edict of Nantes. 'A most esteemed and often quoted work' (Walker).

450   -   ANT

---

39   BBKA *Modern Beekeeping*

349   1880   1904   9th reprinted   Nicely re-bound

A handbook for cottagers.Ran to 10 issues to 1904. Regularly recommended by British Beekeepers' Journal (BBJ), founded 1873. It has a portrait of President of BBKA (1874-1903)Baroness Burdett-Coutts an eminent Victorian philanthropist. She was the wealthiest woman in England. Her father founded Coutts Bank. She established the NSPCC and backed the RSPCA. Contains advertisements by Herrod and Sladen.

20   -   OLD

Geoffrey Lawes

40   BBKA *Modern Beekeeping*

349   1880   1903   9th   Limp copy. Reading copy.

This book, together with Cowan's Guide was the main mode of
instruction by the BBJ,intended to popularise beekeeping in
Britain for the benefit of 'the working class' and intended to wean
them off skeps and on to bar-frame hives with standard frames
and probably also off Karl Marx, Chartism and the worst excesses
of the French Revolution-as Wilde put it.The looming menace to
the well-being of the prosperous middle classes by the growing
population of under-privileged and under-skilled people was to be
met,on the one hand,by convictions,deportation, emigration and
the workhouse, and on the other, by Christian instruction, basic
education and genuine philanthropy. Hence the frequency of
Victorian bee-books addressed to Cottagers to lead them to
useful,unthreatening and profitable pursuits "Middle class
morality?...Morals,Guvnor, can't afford 'em" (Bernard Shaw) as
the skeppist might have said to the reformer. The answer to that
was the supposedly cheap 'Cottager Hive' Though priced at £1 it
still cost well over a week's total wages for a farm worker.

15   -   OLD

SINGLEWALLED "COTTAGER" HIVE
(Butler)

41   BBKA *Beecraft*

-       1965/67   -   -   28 issues in a folder

Aug 1965-Dec 1967

40   -   MOD

42a   BBKA *Beecraft*

-       1968/2001-   -

Sorted into year sets. A total of 408 issues (plus 146 duplicates).Not a complete run but lacks only 16 of the monthly
booklets altogether. Older style small format. From 1980 to 1986 the booklets are nicely bound in 7 BBKA binders.

350   -   MOD

42b   BBKA *Beecraft*

-       2002/2009   -   -   -

January to January. Modern larger format. 63 issues plus 4 duplicates. Approx 15 missing.

50   -   MOD

42c   BBKA *The Beekeeper's Annual*

-       1984-7 and1992   -   -   -

6 issues edited by John Phipps and David Charles. Details of Associations, advice and diary.

10   -   20ᵗʰC

42d   BKA's *Year Books*

-       -   -

Kent-1930, Bucks-1983, Centenary BBKA -1974

8   -   20ᵗʰC

43a   BKAs *Beecraft (early)*
-          -   -   -   (4 copies in all)

Kent and Surrey BKAs only. Manley argues vigorously for his 16x10 inch frames

5   -   20thC

43b   BKAs *Beecraft*
-                    -   -   (9 copies in all)

Now includes Hants. and Glos. Jan 1925 to Jun 1925, then Dec '25,Nov '27 and Oct '31 - by then including 4 more county associations. Some interesting articles and correspondence.

5   -   20thC

43c   BKAs *The beekeepers' record*
-          -   1925   -   (11 monthly issues - March missing)

Book reviews, articles, some interesting photographs and the death of Queen Alexandra.

5   -   20thC

44   Beck, B F   *Honey & Your Health*
554 j53   1947 US1938   -   1st   dw

with D.Smedley. 12 plates. A nutrimental,medicinal and historical commentary

15   -   20thC

45   Beckley, P   *Keeping Bees*
-          1977   -   1st   dw

Garden Farming Series. A user-friendly novice's book promoting the National Hive.

10   -   MOD

46   Beckley, P   *Another*
-          1977   1982   -   pb

-8   -   MOD

47   Bee Research Association   *History of the B R Assoc*
561   1974   -   1st   -

1949-1974: a history of the first 25 years

10   -   20thC

48   Bent, E R   *A Beekeepers Progress*
564   1950   -   1st   (2 copies-1 with dw)

Bibliography pps 40-48 of 36 books plus journals and periodicals. A general discussion of the management of bees and problems that must be considered.

15   2   20thC

49   Bent, E R   *Swarm Control Survey*
563   1946   -   1st   Fair-chipped dw (2 copies)

An excellent summary of methods of controlling the major problem in bee management-the swarming urge. Foreword by Snelgrove.

12   2   20thC

50   Betts, Annie *Practical Bee Anatomy*

501   1923   -   1st   Nice clean copy

with notes on the embryology,metamorphoses etc.1884-1961.Editor Bee World 1929-49. An aeronautical engineer in WW1,researcher into beehive fungus, a linguist and translator of foreign papers. Her detailed account of microscopic techniques gave an easy aid to non-scientific beekeepers" notes Ron Brown.

15   -   20thC

---

51   Betts, Annie *Another*

501   1923   -   1st   Spine bare-

10   -   20thC

---

52   Betts, Annie *The Diseases of Bees: Their Signs, Causes & Treatment*

565   1934   1951   2nd   Pamphlet.

Pub by Hickmont and Co for the Author. "Very clear accounts of signs, causes and treatments…plainly stated commonsense…still worth reading today. (Brown)

12   -   20thC

---

53   Betts, Annie *Another*

565   1934   1951   2nd   Pamphlet

8   -   20thC

---

54   Bevan, Edward   *The Honey Bee*

201   1827   1838   -   Spine a mite loose..

Its natural history, physiology and management. 'Practised as Doctor at Mortlake and at Congleton. His health giving way….retired to Bridstow where he began to study bees. His book…. brought him into correspondence with the foremost beekeepers of his time'. He kept 7 stocks in a beehouse and used bars on his 12 inch square boxes. 'A kind genial man' (Walker). 'He was years ahead of his time and his original book is still valuable for its content, quite apart from its value as an antique' (Ron Brown). Second edition dedicated to Queen Victoria with whom he draws an analogy with a queen bee

120   -   ANT

---

55   Bevan, Edward   *Another*

201   1827   1838   -   -   -

125   -   ANT

---

56   Bevan, Edward   *Another*

201   1827   1870   -   Revised, enlarged and illustrated by W.A. Munn. 12 superb

coloured plates.   -

120   -   ANT

57   Binding, G *About Pollen*

566   1971   1977   5th   pb

Pub Thorsons 'About' Series. A world-wide survey of the uses of pollen.

5   -   MOD

58 Birch, M *Pheromones*

| | 1974 | 1974 | 1st | dw |

North Holland Research Monograph. Univ of California,Davis. Chemical communication in insects and vertebrates explored in depth.

| 30 | - | USA |

---

59 Bonner, James *A New Plan*

| 151 | 1795 | - | 1st | Uncut. Handsomely rebound |

:for speedily increasing the number of beehives in Scotland. Pub. J. Moir and others. 'Bee-Master at Auchencrow, near Berwick. The most able…. of Scottish bee-men' (Walker). He made practical use of Schirack's theory that queens could be raised from worker eggs.

| 420 | - | ANT |

---

60 Bonsels, W *Adventures of Maya the Bee*

| 495 J64 | 1922 | - | 1st | Hardback. Little rubbed. |

For children. Coloured frontispiece by H. Boss

| 10 | - | USA |

---

61 Bonsels, W *Another*

| 495 J64 | 1922 | 1946 | 3rd | Soiled spine. Book plate - a Junior school prize |

Hutchinson's Books for Young People. Translated from German. Clever illustrations. In 1946 the US Army permitted a German printer to reproduce the US 1922 translation.

| 10 | - | 20thC |

---

62 Borror & DeLong *An Introduction to the Study of Insects*

| | 1954 | 1966 | Revised | Large near-mint tome |

A scholarly work on the taxonomy of insects. 98 pps of exact information on the order hymenoptera.

| 25 | - | USA |

---

63 Bradley, Richard *A General Treatise of Husbandry and Gardening*

| 80 | 1721 | 1757 | - | 9 0f the 20 plates lacking Plate 3 is of bees. Torn leather to back cover. |

Originally issued in monthly parts. Corrected and properly methodised. Johnson and Baldwin. An early treatise on bee anatomy. An account of bees,mainly from Maraldi's Memoirs, Paris 1712 (an astronomer) whose work "contains the first accounts of many features of bee life which we now take for granted" (Fraser).

| 120 | - | ANT |

---

64 Brekelmans, T *Skep Making*

| | 1979 | - | 1st | Mint pb in German |

The photos explain how to do it.

| 4 | - | FOR |

---

65 Brett,Walter *Honey from Your Garden*

| 569 | 1940 | 1941 | Reprint | pb |

a handy guide to beekeeping. Food growing Handbooks No 3. "War Time Beekeeping is a National Service" by the Editor of "The Smallholder"

| 6 | - | 20thC |

66 Brett, Walter *Another*

| 569 | 1940 | 1942 | Reprint | Paperback | - |

| 6 | - | 20 |

---

67 Bromwich, Bryan J'Anson *The Experienced Bee Keeper*

| 138 | 1783 | 1783 | 2nd | Bound with D Wildman (see 788) |

A clergyman. He was the first to discover the possibility of keeping more than one queen in a hive. Fertile queens can live together but virgins provoke fighting. This may have prompted the Wells Hive of 1896.(from Fraser) He believed wax was made from pollen.

| 250 | - | ANT |

---

68 Brown, H *The Bee Melody*

| 502 | j70 inUS | 1923 | - | 1st | (3 copies -one signed Tickner Edwardes) |

"A somewhat fanciful book with interesting (classical) quotations and references" (IBRA)

| 18 | 3 | 20thC |

---

69 Brown, Ron *Great Masters of Beekeeping*

| - | 1994 | - | 1st | Mint. |

A thoroughly researched tribute to 30 famous apicultural celebrities, spanning three centuries. 15 half-tone portraits and a bibliography of their writings.

| 10 | - | BAB |

---

70 Brown, Ron *Another*

| - | 1994 | - | 1st | Mint. | - |

| 10 | - | BAB |

---

71 Brown, Ron *Beekeeping, A Seasonal Guide*

| - | 1986 | - | 1st | Mint. Frontispiece by the vendor. |

West Country author (OBE). An engineer and scientist but also a precise and lucid stylist on beekeeping topics, informed by 50 years experience at home and abroad. Takes a seasonal approach explaining management techniques appropriate to the time.

| 20 | - | MOD |

---

72 Brown, Ron *One Thousand Years of Devon Beekeeping*

| 571 | 1975 | - | 1st | pbs (2 copies) |

Features Bro Adam, Woodbury and others.

| 5 | 2 | MOD |

---

73 Brown, Ron *Honeybees. A Guide to Management*

| - | 1988 | - | 1st | Mint |

An excellent guide for novices. Very practical on how to handle equipment.

| 15 | - | MOD |

---

74 Brown, Ron *Beeswax*

| - | 1981 | - | 1st | pb |

The first major work on the subject since Cowan(1908) All one needs to know of the history,collection and uses of beeswax.

8   -   MOD

---

75   Brown, Ron   *Beeswax*

-      1981   -   1st   Mint. Hardback.   -

9   -   MOD

---

76   Brown, Ron   *Simple 2 Queen System*

-      1980   -   1st   pb booklet

16 pps. Based on a lecture given at the Honey Show in 1980. Hive management in succession to Virgil, Wells (1896) and Dugat.

2   -   MOD

---

77   Browning, G   *The Children's Storybook of Bees*

572   1933   -   1st   Rare

6 plates. A children's book for good readers with proper information woven into the life of the hive.

25   -   20thC

---

78   Buckley, Arabella (Mrs Fisher) *Insect Life*

344   1880's   no date   -   .Limp

Intended for clever children. Limited bee matter. A school reader. 8 attractive coloured plates

20   -   OLD

---

79   Budd, Mavis   *The Little Honey Book*

-      1984   -   1st   Mint.   A neat little book. Honey in cooking, drinks and as a remedy for ills

8   -   20thC

---

80   Burch,D V   *Scent Direction of Honeybees*

-      -   1966   -   BRA pamphlet -lecture(2 copies)

International Symposium on Pollination London 1964

4   2   20thC

81a   Burke, P W *Bee Diseases & Pests*

-      1980's   -   no date   Booklet. Canadian.

Excellent coloured photographs of normal and diseased cells.

5   -   USA

81b   Burtt & son *Beekeepers Supplies*

-      1940   1940   -   -

Austerity wartime catalogue. Favours 'regular customers due to shortages.
Running out of red cedar'.

10   -   MISC

82   Busch, Wilhelm   *Buzz-a-Buzz*

324   1872   -   1st   Back cover detached and spine bare,o/w good

The Bees, done freely into English from the German by WC Cotton, author of ' My Bee Book'. Childrens' verse, richly illustrated with amusing drawings

40   -   OLD

83   Busch, Wilhelm   *Buzz-a-Buzz*

324   1872   1983 reprint   -   Mint

Contains an appreciation of Cotton by V. Dodd

20   -   OLD

---

84   Butler,Dr C G   *The Honeybee an Introduction*

577   1949   -   -   (3 copies)

to her sense, physiology and behaviour, by the Cambridge University entomologist. First whiteflies then locusts interested him before becoming the leading figure at Rothamsted.He identified the vital pheremone "queen substance" produced in the mandibular glands.A Fellow of the Royal Society and awarded the OBE.

15   3   20thC

---

85   Butler, Dr C G   *The World of the Honeybee*

578   1954   1967   -

New Naturalist Series No 29. 2 col and 87 other photographs. "A classic for all times most strongly recommended to beekeepers and anyone else"(Brown)"

20   -   20thC

---

86   Butler,Dr C G   *Another*

578   -   1971   Fair. Ex library copy   -

10   -   20thC

---

87   Butler,Dr C G   *Another*

578   -   1976   -   -

20   -   20thC

---

88   Butler,Dr C G   *Another*

578   -   1977   -   -

20   -   20thC

---

89   Butler,Rev Charles
The Feminine Monarchie

18   1609   1623   -   -

:or The Historie of bees. Written out of experience. John Haviland for Roger Jackson and ' to be sold at his shop in Fleet Street'. Dedicated to Henrietta Maria, consort of Charles I. The 'most readable edition'. Contains a four part 'Bees madrigal printed so that the singers facing each other two and two might each hold the book and sing his part'. (Walker) 'The greatest early British Bee Book.... the best account of skep bee-keeping which is available today'. Butler (1571-1647) was a clergyman, keen to collect his tithes and a musicologist and advocate of phonetic spelling. The window of his church (Wootton St.Lawrence) is pictured by Ron Brown (on his dust wrapper) and

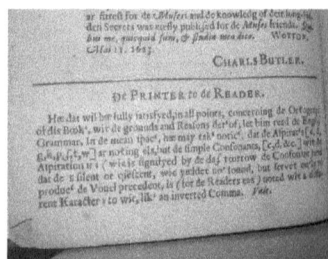

Daphne More (731).

475   -   ANT

---

90   Butler,Rev Charles   *Another*

18   1609   1634   3rd   -

Wm Turner for the Author. Phonetic spelling throughout devised by Butler in his 'The English Grammar', Oxford,1633.

650   -   ANT

---

91   Butler,Rev Charles   *Another*

18   1609   1985   -   Reprint of 1623 edition. Cased -

35   -   ANT

---

92   Buzzard, C N   *Shining Hours*

581   1946   -   1st   dw

Illustrated by J Yunge-Bateman with fine drawings. Beekeeping experiences and experiments in Southern France

9   -   20thC

---

93   Buzzard, C N   *Another*

581   -   1946   1st   No dw -

8   -   20thC

---

94   Buzzard, C N   *Another*

581   1946   1952   1st reprint dw

8   -   20thC

---

95   Buzzard, C N   *Another*

581   -   -   1st reprint No dw

4   -   20thC

---

96   Calder, A   *Oilseed Rape & Bees*

-   1986   -   1st   (3 copies) pbs

The widely-grown new crop with advantages and problems for beekeepers. "Honey as white as milk" 53 references in bibliography

8   3   MOD

---

97   Calder, Margaret   *Honey Favourites*

-   1983   -   1st   28 page pamphlet

A duplicated booklet of recipes.

8   -   MOD

---

98   Calhoun, L *A Lifetime with Bees*

-   1979   -   1st   pb

Starts with an interesting autobiograhical note.by a N. Carolina hobbyist and teacher.. Modest photos and an easy style.

8   -   USA

99   Callahan,Philip C *Insect Behavior*
-        1970   -   1st   dw
Prof of Entomology, Univ.of Florida. Tips on studying insect behaviour and using photography
15   -   USA

100   Campion, A *Bees at the Bottom of the Garden*
-        1984   -   1st   pb (2 copies)
Intended to encourage the potential hobbyist by describing hive management. Artistically illustrated.
9   2   MOD

101   Carter, G   *The Hive Bee*
584   1948   -   1st   (4 copies all with dws)
12 plates. "Written for the lover of nature,not as a manual" (Wadey") Mr Carter produced films about bees and
beekeeping too.
12   4   20thC

102   Carter, G   *Bees & Honey*
583   1946   -   2nd   (3 copies) :
a guide to the better understanding of bees, their diseases and the chemistry of beekeeping. Concise, user-friendly
with the author's helpful photographs.
10   3   20thC

103   Carter, G   *Another*
583   1945   -   1st   (2 copies)   -
10   2   20thC

104   Cartland, Barbara *The Magic of Honey*
585   1970   -   -   Paperback Recipes.
"It is important for sex, for a balanced mind, and a happy intellect"
5   -   20thC

105   Cartland, Barbara *Another*
585   1970   -   -   Paperback   -
5   -   20thC

106   Chambers – Publishers, *The Bee*
-        1841-2   -   -   In a modern card wrap
No 61 information for the people. 16pages. An informative article covering many aspects of bee husbandry.
15   -   ANT

107   Chapman, A Darcy   *A Honeybee and her Master*
587   1936   1944   -   (2 copies) reprint dws
For children. A most engaging work combining an entertaining account of bees with sound scientific and biological
information as befitted a teacher of Method at a Teachers' Training College
9   2   20thC

108   Cheshire, Frank   *Bees & Beekeeping*

388   1886   -   1st   Vol 1 Scientific

:a complete treatise on the anatomy,physiology,floral relations and profitable management of the hive bee..Pub Upcott Gill with 14pps of adverts for their 'Practical Handbooks' etc. Cheshire was a schoolmaster,microscopist and discoverer of the cause of foul brood. 'The standard English textbook for at least forty years...far in advance of any previous book both in matter and arrangement' (Fraser)

60   -   OLD

---

109   Cheshire, Frank   *Another*

388   1886   1888   -   Vol 2 Practical   -

60   -   OLD

---

110   Cheshire, Frank   *Another*

388   1886   -   1st   Volume 1 Scientific.. Gilt stamped. V clean copy   -

40   -   OLD

---

111   Chitty, W   *Beekeeping for Beginners*

424   1903   1903   1st

:according to the syllabus of the Board of Education. He was a'Day School Teacher' - but incudes recipes for making mead. 4 pps of adverts.

25   -   OLD

---

112   Chitty, W   *Another*

424   1903   1903   1st

25   -   OLD

---

113   Chylinski, Dobrogost   *The Beekeepers Manual*

251   1845   -   later ed   Small limp version.Frontispiece but no other plates mentioned in the text.

Industrial Library. Advocates the large Polish upright hive (3 to 5 feet high). 'The world is a school and all nature is a schoolmaster' An interesting essay on a truly moral education based on experience rather than dogmatic instruction.

35   -   ANT

---

114   Clark, K K   *Beekeeping*

590   1951   -   1st   (5 copies) pb

Penguin Books. Meant for amateurs and hobbyists to highlight common best practice.

5   5   20thC

---

115   Clegg, J   *Insects*

-        1957   -   -   Chipped dw

A general work. An informative account targeted on learners of all ages as appropriate by the Curator of Haslemere Educational Museum

5   -   20thC

116 Clements, D   *Gale the Man & the Business*

| - | 1986 | - | 1st | Paperback booklet |

About AW Gale, a remarkable character. 1900-1969 Commercial beekeeping from home and abroard.Duplicated script. Generous foreword by Bro Adam.

| 2 | - | MOD |

---

117 Clemson, Alan   *Honey & Pollen Flora*

| - | 1985 | - | 1st | Mint |

Australian. A beautiful book. 90 pps on the eucalypts.

| 30 | - | MOD |

---

118 Cloudsley-Thompson   *Bees & Wasps*

| 591 | 1974 | - | 1st |

Bodley Head New Biology. For children Uncomplicated information interestingly presented by Prof. of Zoology, Birkbeck College. London.

| 8 | - | 20ᵗʰC | - |

---

119 Cobbett, William *Cottage Economy*

| 189 | 1822 | 1831 | - |

Cobbett urges poor cottagers to keep bees (Section 160 to 166)as well as pigs,cows etc. 'Scarcely anything is a greater misfortune than shiftlessness'

| 60 | - | ANT |

---

120 Cockerell,Prof TDA   *African Bees*

| 591a | 1937 | - | 1st |

British Museum.. Bees of the genera Ceratina, Halictus and Megachile. Prof. Emeritus of Zoology

| 30 | - | 20ᵗʰC |

---

121 Collings, A *Candle Making*

| - | 1971 | - | 1st reprint Paperback, 32 pages Uses paraffin wax as well as beeswax |

| 5 | - | 20ᵗʰC |

---

122 Columella, Lucius *Of Husbandry*

| 98 | 1745 | - | 1st | In 12 books |

In 12 books, translated by Curtius. Columella, a Spaniard, wrote about a century after Virgil. 'Probably a commercial beekeper...gave advice on apiary management including requeening,uniting and migratory beekeeping' (Fraser). Index has 10 entries on bees. A well-preserved large book.

| 350 | - | ANT |

---

123 Comstock, Anna *How to Keep Bees*

| 429 J101 | 1905 | 1907 | - |

:a handbook for the use of beginners. 1854-1930. Professor at Cornell Univ. In 1923 she was named as one of the greatest women in the USA to that date. Good photos and a critical bibliography of US books.

| 30 | - | USA |

124 Cook, A J *Bee-Keepers' Guide or Manual of the Apiary*

J103   1876   1882   7th   Slightly cracked,spine rubbed.

Walker included 4 editions in his 1929 collection. Never published in the UK. In two parts,- natural history and the apiary.Illustrated by 133 drawings.

50   -   USA

125 Cook, A J *Another*

J103   1876   1884   11th   Revised and enlarged

"The most extensive of all the beekeeping manuals written for American beekeepers…a most excellent teacher at the Univ of Michigan" (Comstock)

50   -   USA

126 Cook, A J *Another*

J103   1876   1894   15th   Revised and enlarged

17th Thousand' 11pps of period advertisements.

50   -   USA

127 Cook, Vince *Queen Rearing Simplified*

-    1986   -   1st   pb

A modern expert.He had commercial experience in New Zealand ,here applied to queen-rearing by grafting. Very helpful photographs.

9   -   MOD

128 Cooke, Samuel   *The Complete English Gardener & the Complete Beemaster*

133   1780   2nd   Cropped margins. Bees in pps 86 -105

A gardener at Overton, Wiltshire. A skeppist who advocates killing the bees to take the honey.

150   -   ANT

129 Cooper, Beowulf *The Honeybees of the British Isles*

-    1986   -   -   Unbound review proof copy.With Denwood's letter to Dodd

He had a profound belief in the value of the traditional(and largely lost) British Black Bee. Cooper was an entomologist who died in 1982. His unedited material was reorganised into book form by Philip Denwood.

15   -   MOD

130 Cooper, Beowulf *The Hymenopterist's Handbook*

-    1943   1945   1st   pb loose cover

Edited by the leading advocate of British Black bees. See also MOD 129"The Amateur Entomologist" Vol 7 No 40. Ingenious devices and specialist classifications. 20 contributions.

20   -   20thC

131 Corner, J *Beehive Construction*

-    1976   -   -   Booklet

Canadian and N America style hives

5   -   USA

132   Cotton, W C *My Bee Book*

238	1842	1842	1st	Rebound

Original irregular pagination. A diverse collection of letters to cottagers,poems and reprinted extracts from older writers together with Cotton's ideas on developing beekeeping in New Zealand. Advocates puff-ball narcotic to save the bees' lives. Many woodcuts by W Whimper. See also No 788 for his 'Letter to Cottagers'.

250	-	ANT

133a Cotton, W C *Another*

238	1842	1842	1st	Spine bumped
200	-	ANT		

133b Cotton, W C *Another*

238	1842	1842	1st	Poor condition but complete ready for rebinding.
100	-	ANT		

134   Cotton, W C *Another*

238	1842	1970	-	Reprint. dw chipped

Modern copy

15	-	ANT

135   Cotton, W C A *Manual for N Z Beekeepers*

651	1848	1976	-	Reprint. Cloth

Wellington, New Zealand. No 651, one of a limited edition of only 850, 'bound in Almond Kivar bookcloth'.

25	-	ANT

136   Coult, D A *Molecules & Cells*

-	1970?	-	-	pb Plain cover

Scientific textbook. The basic chemistry of living matter,protoplasm and the cell

15	-	MISC

137   Couston, R *Principles of Practical Beekeeping*

594	1972	-	1st	dw (2 copies)

Beekeeping Advisor for the East of Scotland. A practical guide "in short, racy style"

8	2	20thC

138   Couston, R *Another*

594	1972	-	1st	Signed by author
-12	-	20thC		

139 Cowan and William Broughton Carr
British Bee Journal

- 1891 - - Bound copies.

The BBJ published continuously from 1874,in the main as a
weekly paper working in close association with the BBKA
which was founded in 1874 following an inaugural
exhibition and competition at the Crystal Palace as part of
the National Dary Show. Mr. Cowan, Chairman BBKA, and
WBC were joint editors of these volumes of the weekly
publication.

45 - OLD

140 Cowan and William Broughton Carr *Another*

- 1892 - - -

45 - OLD

---

141 Cowan and William Broughton Carr *Another*

- 1893 - - -

45 - OLD

---

142 Cowan and William Broughton Carr *Another*

- 1894 - - -

45 - OLD

---

143 Cowan and William Broughton Carr *Another*

- 1895 - - Has obituary of Langstroth

45 - OLD

---

144 Cowan and William Broughton Carr *Another*

- 1896 - - -

45 - OLD

---

145 Cowan,Thomas W *British Beekeepers Guide Book*

356   1881   1896   14th   hb v clean :

the management of bees in moveable frame hives and the use of the extractor."Far in advance of any books except
Cheshire's…a model of system,conciseness and comprehensiveness"(Fraser) Translated into seven languages.
"Through the influence of this little guide…the form of British bee-keeping practice took on its well-known
characteristics" (Manley)

25   5   OLD

146a Cowan,Thomas W *Another*

356   1881   1898   15th   White printed cover

Understandably this book was enthusiastically promoted by the BBJ

20   OLD

---

147 Cowan, Thomas W *The Honey Bee*

404   1890   1890   1st   Others

:its natural history,anatomy and physiology. Advanced advice. Fraser points to an error in that larvae are not fed on regurgitated food,but says the book was singularly well adapted for its time.

15   -   OLD

---

148 Cowan, Thomas W *Another*

404   1890   1890   1st   Gilt stamped

About the anatomy. Grimshaw in a contemporary review says "To take the whole literature on the science of bee life…(in 5 languages)…and marshall all that is worth knowing in a straightforward,simple and compact way is a task of almost Herculean mental magnitude…(so)accomplished that (I pronounce it)…far and away the finest book…yet published on the life-history of the honey-bee".

20   -   OLD

---

149 Cowan, Thomas W *Another*

404   1890   1904   2nd   (3 copies)

3   15   OLD

---

150 Cowan, Thomas W *Another*

404   1890   1904   2nd   Signed Tickner Edwardes   -

20   -   OLD

---

151 Cowan, Thomas W *BBK Assoc Jubilee*

595   1928   1928   1st   Harrison Ashworth's copy

History of the Association representing 50 years of beekeeping progress. Fascinating items and photographs from the BBJ

40   -   20thC

---

152 Cowan, T W *Waxcraft*

442   1908   -   1st   one paper cover loose

:all about beeswax,its history,production,adulteration and commercial value. 17 plates. Said to be the only major work on the subject till Ron Brown's 'Beeswax (1981)

30   -   OLD

---

153 Cowan, T W *Another*

442   1908   -   1st   -   -

30   -   OLD

---

154 Cowan, T W *Another*

442   1908   -   1st   -   -

25   -   OLD

---

155 Cowan, Thomas W *British Beekeepers Guide Book*

356   1881   -   24th   Tickner Edwardes' own copy   -

20   -   OLD

---

156   Crane, Dr Eva   *Honey, A Comprehensive Survey*

603   1975   1979   3rd   dw. With corrections.

The doyen of British beekeeping.OBE died 2007. Director of IBRA 1948,"One of the largest stores of beekeeping knowledge ever held under one roof…under her far-seeing and brilliant motivation" (Stevens). A prolific author of classic definitive academic work. This book is a library of contributions by many expert hands.

45   -   MOD

---

157   Crane, Dr Eva   *The Archaeology of Beekeeping*

-      1983   -   1st

An comprehensive account of beekeeping world-wide and from time immemorial

90   -   MOD

---

158   Crane, Dr Eva   *Dictionary of Beekeeping Terms (Scandinavia)*

599   1971   Vol. 1V   -   -

Part of a major enterprise to facilitate international understanding of beekeeping words. E.g.HIVE stade (Dan) kube(Nor) bikupe(Swe)

10   -   BAB

---

159   Crane, Dr Eva   *Dictionary of Beekeeping Terms (Italian & Spanish)*

599   1958   Vol. 11   -

E.g DRONE fuco(Ital) Zangano(Span)

10   -   BAB

---

160   Crane, Dr Eva   *A Book of Honey*

-      1980   -   1st   pb (2 copies)

A diverting exploration of honey - raw materials,uses and applications,history and its part in the spiritual life of mankind. Also scientific data and a bibliography.

12   2   MOD

---

161   Crane, E & Townsend   *Index to Apicultural Abstracts*

-      1976   -   1st   2 volumes

Tools for researchers

40   -   BAB

---

162   Croft, Dr L *Profitable Beekeeping*

-      1986   -   1st   (2 copies)

Probably over-optimistic encouragement for people seeking financial rewards as well as satisfaction from the craft. Covers economic practice and saleale products other than honey.

15   2   MOD

---

163   Croft, Dr L *Curiosities of Beekeeping*

-      1989   1990   2nd   Paperback

A miscellany of myths,marvels and memorable matters from the annals of beekeeping. Pub NBB

4   -   MOD

164   Crompton, J   *The Hunting Wasp*

-        1948   -   1st   -

Pseudonym -John Lamburn. Mainly about wasps but Chap. 3 concerns wasps that hunt for bees.

12   -   20thC

---

165   Crompton, J   *The Hive*

605   1947   -   1st   (4 copies all with dws)

Illustrated by AE Bestall. A collection of stories about bees and their behaviour

15   4   20thC

---

166   Crompton, J   *The Hive of Bees*

-        1958   -   US ed   dw

A pseudonym for John Lamburn, a big game hunter retired to Kent "If you wish to call me an anthropomorphist you may" He takes a sensitive approach to a bee's experiences!.

15   -   USA

---

167   Crosse, RTS
The Hive & Its Wonders

274' j111 1852 1851   1876   -

Smaller brown version

Religious Tract Society.Originally written for children
for the American Sunday School Union

25   -   OLD

---

168   Crosse, RTS   *Another*

274   1852   1853   New and revised   very clean copy

Excellent illustrations including a bee farm,cottagers' hives and hunting stingless bees

30   -   OLD

---

169   Crosse, RTS   *Another*

274   1852   1853   -   slightly rubbed   -

25   -   OLD

---

170   Crowder, D E   *The Flying Nation*

607   1951   -   1st   (3 copies- 1 with torn dw)

Illust Helen Haywood. For children with 8 col plates. "It has personalised bees but no young people…
no moralising…or overtly Christian message" (Showler)

12   3   20thC

---

171   Cumming & Logan   *Beekeeping Craft & Hobby*

609   1950   -   1st   (4 copies 3 with dws)

16 plates. Favours the Glen Hive with 15 frames in each box. Meant for small-scale beekeepers offering sound, clear advice on well-established Scottish lines.

15   4   20thC

172 Cumming, A R   *Northern Beekeeper*

| 608 | 1942 | 1945 | 2nd | Paperback: |

handbook of the Inverness BKA. Illustrated. "An elementary guide to crofters" The collective wisdom of the Inverness-shire BKA made readily available

| 10 | - | 20ᵗʰC |

---

173 Cumming, Rev John   *Beekeeping (by The Times Beemaster)*

| 304 | 1864 | 1864 | 1st | By The Times beemaster |

A Scottish Minister of Religion. The book reflects controversial newspaper correspondence with Tegetmeier, a pigeon expert, whose collection of bee books passed via Albert Neighbour to Col. Walker in 1890. Cumming opposed moveable-frame hives (too expensive for cottagers), disapproved of sulphuring bees and won good yields of honey from Stewarton or Ayrshire Hives at Tunbridge Wells. He also advocated bell-glasses.

| 75 | - | OLD |

---

174 Cumming, Rev John   *Beekeeping (by The Times Beemaster)*

| 304 | 1864 | 1864 | 1st | Fair. Cover loose, spine cracked. | - |

| 50 | - | OLD |

---

175 Cumming, Rev John   *Another*

| 304 | 1864 | 1871 | 2nd | Fair. Cover loose, spine cracked. |

By the Times Beemaster.

| 50 | - | OLD |

---

176 Curnuck, K   *Floral Decorations in Wax*

| - | - | - | - | Leaflet |

10 page printed pamphlet giving basic guidance on wax-flower making.

| 2 | - | MOD |

---

177 Dadant (Grout)   *The Hive and the Honeybee*

| J284 | 1946 | - | 1st issue | (2 copies -1 with torn dw the other issued in London in 1947) |

The revised edition was the work of 13 co-authors. The tome is an absolute mine of information on all aspects of its original title The Dadants were Charles(1817-1902) and son Camille(1851-1938). They adopted an 11-frame brood box modified by Pellett. In 1855 Langstroth entrusted Dadant with the updating of his book which by then had been reprinted 20 times and was 'dated'. The subsequent monumental revision has been updated ever since and translated into five other languages by Dadant & Sons of Hamilton, Illinois. Premier appliance manufacturing company in the world, a family business begun by Charles Dadant who emigrated from France . They published the American Bee Journal and issued over 30 editions of this book since Langstroth's first in 1853. The firm maintain a fine library of bee books. The modified Dadant hive is the largest standard hive in use today.

| 30 | - | USA |

---

178 Dadant   *Another*

| J284 | 1975 | 1978 | 4th printing | Revised |

Edited by Dadant with a staff of 27 specialists

| 15 | - | USA |

179   Dadant, C P *Dadant System of Beekeeping*
J121   1920   1920   1st   Signed by Sturges
Very good period photographs and illustrations. Tells of their many experiments with hive and frame sizes and how they came to adopt the frame of Moses Quinby.
50   -   USA

180   Dadant, C P *First Lessons in Beekeeping*
J120   1917   1917   1st Revised   Signed Edwardes.
"A short treatise for beginners" Well illustrated
50   -   USA

181   Dade, H A   *Anatomy & Dissection of the Honeybee*
611   1962   -   1st   -
Bee Research Association. 20 pull-out plates and bibliography.1897-1979. WW1 service as a Major followed by agricultural research in Ghana, then Kew in 1935. Leading roles in the Quekett Microscopical Club in the 50's and the BRA. The pre-eminent anatomist of our times.
35   -   20thC

182   Dade, H A   *Another*
611   1962   -   1st   -   -
35   -   20thC

183   Dade, H A   *The Lab Diagnosis of Honeybee Diseases*
610   1949   1949   1st   -
Monographs of the Quekett Micro Club No 4. Useful guidance for the amateur microscopist.
15   -   20thC

184   Dade, H A   *Another*
610   1948   1949   Revised   Pamphlet   -
10   -   20thC

185   Davis, G   *Beekeeping in the Swarming Season*
612   1976   1980   Revised   Paperback
A practical man's straightforward advice on dealing with colonies that want to reproduce themselves and how to manage "making increase".
8   -   20thC

186   de Gelieu, Jonas   *The Bee Preserver*
204   1829   -   1st   Uncut. Original boards
Practical directions for the management and preservation of bees. Translated from the French by Miss Stirling Graham. 'A work of great repute' (Walker)
130   -   ANT

187   De Ribeaucourt, C   *A Manual of Rational Beekeeping*

346   1879   -   1st   Scarce

Translated by Leveson-Gower. Pub Diprose and Bateman An interesting extractor spun with twine (Schmiedl) The frontispiece is a superb coloured design for a bee-house.

50   -   OLD

---

188   Deans   *The Beekeepers Encylopaedia*

613   1949   -   1st   (7 copies)

14 plates. Right Way Books. A short Scottish bee manual. Not alphabetical despite title. Frontispiece shows Deans with King George VI.

5   7   20thC

---

189   Deans, A S C   *Bees & Beekeeping*

615   1962   -   1st   Rubbed

Quest Library. For children in accessible language. Sound information and encouraging for young beekeepers, especially the 'Do-it-Yourself' section.

8   -   20thC

---

190   Deans. A S C   *Beekeeping Techniques*

616   1963   -   1st

Scientific and statistical principles applied to beekeeping issues.

40   -   20thC

191a Diemer, Irmgard *Bees and Beekeeping*

-       1988   -   1st   (4 copies)

American translation of a German text, edited by the vendor into an English context who also devised the illustrations to accompany it. 'Its German provenance does not show as the editorial process has smoothed away any infelicities' (Bee Craft)" Profuse colour and b&w illustrations"

12   4   MOD

191b Diemer, Irmgard *Bienan*

-       1986   -   1st

Original German text. Different illustrations.

12   MOD

191c Min of Ag   *Leaflets*

-              -

1996-2003 Advice on Varroa,Hive Beetle and Foul brood Disease.

3   MOD

---

192   Digges, Rev Joseph   *The Practical Bee Guide*

428   1910   -   -   (19 copies in total) various dates, editions and conditions. Average price quoted.

First appeared in 1904 as 'The Irish Bee Guide'. Subsequently 16 editions followed, selling 76,000 copies. The 8th and later editions were revised by ROB Manley. He first distinguished two types of wax moth (1936). Digges edited and master-minded the Irish Bee Journal until his death in 1933. Digges was a Director of an Irish coal mine, a railway, a creamery and a cooperative bank, so Showler notes in the Encyclop. of Beekeeping. Copies are 5th hb X 2,7th 1932 hb worn,9th X6 brown 2 poor 1941,11th X 3 red 1943,12th grey,14th X 4 green, 15th and 16th both green.

15   19   OLD

---

193   Dines & Dalton   *Honeybees from Close up*

617   1968   -   1st   (2 copies - 1 with dw)

Brilliant photographs by Stephen Dalton and others.26 cm size. Dines MBE was editor of Bee Craft.

20   2   20thC

---

194   Dodd, V   *Beemasters of the Past*

-   1983   1983   1st   -

A stylish and literate work covering notable apiarians of the 17th to 20th centuries. Many illustrations by Jenny Brown. Pub Northern Bee Books.

10   -   BAB

---

195   Doering, H   *A Bee is Born*

619 J145   1962   -   1stx2. 8thx1   (3 copies)

Translated from German by Dale S Cunningham. For children who appreciate brilliant black and white photographs

10   3   20thC

196   Doering, H   *Die Welt der Beine*

-   1956   1956   1st   Large format German

Superb photos in close-up

30   -   FOR

---

197   Doolittle, G M   *Scientific Queen Rearing*

J148   1888   1889   6th   Limp copy

"The father of modern queen rearing". Invented a mandril for making artificial queen cups and perfected techniques for transferring young larvae into them.

40   -   USA

---

198   Doolittle, G M   *Another*

J148   1888   1889   6th   Limp copy. Spine frayed

25   -   USA   -

---

199   Dublon, C & P   *Practical Queen Rearing*

-   1987   -   -   Signed by author. Spring binding

Clear exposition using the punched cell and Jenter methods of cell-raising.

12   -   MOD

---

200   Duffin, E A   *Beeswax Flower Making*

-   1980's   -   -   Leaflet

An 8 page duplicated guide

2   -   MOD   -

201   Dugat, Fr. M   ***The Skyscraper Hive***

620   1948   -   1st   (4 copies-3 with dws)

Translated by Reeves from French. Father Dugat was a Trappist monk. One photo shows an enormous stack of 7 boxes with 7 queens.

15   4   20thC

---

202   Dunbar, Rev William (Jardine)
The Natural History of Bees

236   1840   1840   1st

30 beautifully coloured plates. Naturalists' Library No XXVI. Entomology Vol VI Dunbar was Minister of Applegarth and disciple of Huber whose life is described in the book. Mainly scientific. Sometimes attributed to Sir William Jardine, the general editor of the series.

250   -   ANT

203a Dunbar, Rev William (Jardine)
The Natural History of Bees

236   1840   1843   3rd   very clean copy

Engraving of Huber as frontispiece and many other excellent illustrations.

175   -   ANT

203b Evelyn, John   *Elysium Britannicum*

1659

Not published. Manuscript only extant. This is a BRA pamphlet. 41pps. Edited with commentary by DA Smith 1965.

5   -   ANT

---

204   Duncan & Duncan   *Bees Wasps and Ants*

460a   1913   -   -

Beautiful book for children. Wonders of Insect Life. Excellent coloured plate of a skep.

20   -   OLD

---

205   Duncan & Duncan   *Another*

460a   1913   1923   -

15   -   OLD

---

206   Duncan & Duncan   *Another*

460a   1913   1925?   -   Limp copy   -

10   -   OLD

---

207   Duncan & Duncan   *Another*

460a   1913   1917   -   Limp copy   -

10   -   OLD

208 Dunning, J M   *The Key to the Hive*

622   1945   -   1st   (2 copies) :

the habits and products of the honey-bee. Kingsgate Press. "The secrets of the apiary applied to the social, political, ethical and spiritual problems of our time" Interesting photographs.

5   2   20ᵗʰC

---

209 Eaton, M   *The Ambrose Colouring Annual*

-        1980's   -   -   Booklet

Cartoons for children to fill in.

2   -   MISC

---

210 Edwardes, Rev Tickner   *Beekeeping Do's & Don'ts*

515   1925   -   1st   Signed by author.

Recommends WBC hive and a black silk veil. Rector of Burpham, Arundel, Sussex -practical as well as literary. "The best known English writer on bees" (Mace)

30   -   20ᵗʰC

---

211 Edwardes, Rev Tickner   *The Beemaster of Warrilow*

439   1907   -   1st   -

"That queer little honey coloured book of far -off days" Edwardes in his preface to 2nd enlarged edition. 'Pleasant and imaginative ; excellent photo' (Walker)

20   -   OLD

---

212 Edwardes, Rev Tickner   *Another*

439   1907   1920   2nd   (2 copies)

The 2nd is nearly three times the length of the first pre-war edition.

15   2   OLD

---

213 Edwardes, Rev Tickner   *Beekeeping for All*

503   1923   -   1st   (2 copies)

:a manual of honeycraft. He invented his own hive - photographed.

15   2   20ᵗʰC

---

214 Edwardes, Rev Tickner   *Another*

503   1923   -   5th/6th/7th,8th editions   (8 copies) Includes 4 of the 9 editions.

"My position is to represent bee-keeping as a profitable sideline" Wadey says of him "stretcher-bearer and later Captain in the RAMC, medical entomologist in the Middle East, at the age of 60 took Holy Orders" The Poet of Beekeeping.

5   8   20ᵗʰC

---

215 Edwardes, Rev Tickner   *The Lore of the Honeybee*

440   1908   1917   8th   Edwardes own copy

A history of bees and their masters from the earliest times…as well as the romance of beemanship past and present. Dedicated to Cowan. 'A wonderful story…told with great charm, and much literary art' (Daily Telegraph) "The best and most informing work on the hive-bee hitherto published. Somewhat in the style of 'La vie des abeilles' but more accurate" (Walker).

20   -   OLD

216 Edwardes, Rev Tickner *Another*
440   1908   -   -   (9 copies - 2nd to 18th -1944) -
15   9   OLD

217 Evans, J and Berrett, Sheila *The Complete Guide*
-    1989   -   1st   (2 copies)
A handsome modern guidebook by a W Sussex beekeeper. Some photographs by the vendor.
16   2   MOD

218 Evrard, E *A Mystery of the Hive*
504 J166 1923   -   1st   One of (2 copies) is a review copy and the other is signed by Arthur Sturges
Translated from French by B.Miall. Philosophical thoughts on the wonders of nature as exemplified by bees.
20   2   20thC

219 Ewald, C *The Battle of the Bees*
-    1977   -   1st   Waterstained. dw. Fair
Stories for children translated and adapted from the Danish of Ewald (1856-1908). An early demonstration of ecological soundness on the balance of nature.
8   -   USA

220 Fabre *The Book of Insects*
-    1912?   -   -   A great book
12 of the famous Detmold plates. Not on bees
70   -   MISC

221 Fabre, J Henri *The Mason Bees*
468   1914   -   1st   Translated by de Mattos
"The mason-bee's sting is far less powerful than that of the hive-bee."
25   -   MISC

222 Fabre, J Henri *Another*
468   1914   -   1st   Cover slightly loose.French Large   -
20   -   MISC

223 Fatigati, Evelyn *Bzzz A Beekeeper's Primer*
-    1976   -   1st   dw
Alan, aged 12, learns about beekeeping from his Granddad. Illustrations by the Iowa author.
10   -   USA

224 Ferrari, Gestaldi *Dalle Api*
-    1969   -   1st   Italian. pb Nice coloured plates. A short guide to apiculture.
8   -   FOR

225 Field, Oliver *Honey by the Ton*

-          1983   -   1st   dw

Beefarming -how to get a living from bees. Trenchant forthright writing in amusing style by "The greater two-footed hive thumper" Much good practical advice. Predates varroa in the UK.

8   -   MOD

226a Figuier, Louis *The Insect World*

312   1868   1872   New and revised   Spine loose. Green copy Dragonfly frontispiece and title page missing

Rev and corrected by PM Duncan. Bees pps313-317. 579 woodcuts. Illustrations of European appliances. Origin Paris 1867

30   -   OLD

226b Figuier, Louis *Another*

312   1868   1872   New and revised   Spine slightly loose Brown cover

30   -   OLD

226c Figuier, Louis *Another*

312   1868   168   1st   Spine a little loose at top and detached o/w very clean and well-bound

:being a popular account of the orders of insects. 564 woodcuts by MM.E.Blanchard. Bees pps 313-371. Many brilliant illustrations on every type of insect

40   -   OLD

---

227 Filleul, Rev P V M *The English Beekeeper*

271   1851   1851   1st

A Country Curate. Another of the legion of clerical gentlemen who kept and wrote about bees. "Quite a good book for its time" (Fraser) 'The greater part of the volume is old matter' (Preface) A few neat woodcuts.

120   -   OLD

---

228 Filleul, Rev P V M *Another*

271   1851   1851   1st   -

120   -   OLD

---

229 Fisher, M *The Beekeepers Annual*

-          1992   -   -   pb   -

5   -   MOD

---

230 Flower, A B *Beekeeping Up-to-date*

516   1925   1930   2nd   Fair dw (2 copies)

Cassells Pet and Livestock Series. Herrod-Hempsall praises her in his foreword for managing many stocks at home and in out-apiaries

10   2   20thC

---

231   Flower, A B   *Another*

516   1925   -   -   (7 copies) Various editions and conditions

Miss Flower's book ran to 8 editions to 1942."This work is neither by a mushroom (?overnight sensation?) nor an armchair beekeeper, but is practical in every way" (H-Hempsall). She favours WBCs, supers and section crates.

3   7   20thC

232   Francis & Gontier   *The Book of Honey*

-        1981   -   1st   Mint hb

A lovely book about honey with 122 pages of recipes

12   -   MOD

233   Francon, Julien   *The Mind of the Bees*

632   1939   -   1st UK edition   (2 copies)

Translated from French by H Eltringham. Bibliography. Concerns experiments to learn of the communication of bees and their behaviour outside the hive.

10   2   20thC

234   Francon, Julien   *Another*

632   1939   -   1st   Gift to T. Edwardes   -

15   -   20thC

235   Francon, Julien   *Another*

632   1939   -   1st   (2 copies) Fair dw   -

12   2   20thC

236   Francon, Julien   *Another*

632   1939   1947   2nd   -   -

10   -   20thC

237a Fraser, H Malcolm   *Beekeeping in Antiquity*

633   1931   1931   1st   Sturges' copy

A scholarly account of classic writers from the earliest times.

45   -   BAB

237b Fraser, H Malcolm   *Another*

633   1931   1951   2nd   Near mint

30   -   BAB

239   Free, Prof JB   *The Social Organisation of Honeybees*

-        1977   -   1st   Small pamphlet

Expert at the Bee Dept. Rothamsted Experimental Station Author of many academic and authoritative books and reports. Tells how bees in a colony interact and communicate to create a coordinated organic whole.

5   -   MOD

240   Free, Prof JB   *Bees & Mankind*

-        1982   -   1st   -

World-wide historical interaction between man and bees. A handsome book with excellent photographs.

15   -   MOD

---

241   Free, Prof JB   *Honeybee Biology*

-     1982   -   -

18 lecures given to the Central Association of Beekeepers by 12 Doctors of Science -Pickard, Butler etc.

20   -   MOD

---

242   Furness, C   *Beeswax Candles*

-     1985?   -   -   pb

A 20 page pamphlet. Revised to include customs, history and judging as well as how to make candles

5   -   MOD

---

243   Furness, C   *Mary Workman's Honey Recipes*

640   1974   1974   1st   Plastic spine binding

Pub by Bee Breeders Assoc. Mary wrote for the BBJ This book of recipes was compiled from her diaries after her death in 1973.

5   -   20thC

---

244   Fussell, George   *The Old English Farming Books*

-     1947   -   1st

:from Fitzherbert to Tull. 1523-1730 The acknowledged expert on agricultural history. Markham, Hartlib and Worlidge treated.

30   -   BAB

---

245   G L C   *Beehive Paintings from Slovenia*

-     1983   -   1st   pb

6 col plates. Janscha (b 1734) was Empress Maria Theresa's Royal Beekeeper and a fine artist.
This booklet accompanied a loan exhibition at the Horniman Museum in1983.

10   -   MOD

---

246   Galton, D   *The Beehive*

-     1982   -   1st   Paperback :

an enquiry into its origins and history. Illustrated, scholarly and authoritative.
Honey gathering world-wide since the stone age.

10   -   MOD

---

247   Galton, D   *Survey of 1,000 Years of Beekeeping in Russia*

641   1971   -   -   Paperback

Pub by BRA. A whole new perspective on the history, art and science of beekeeping.

10   -   20thC

---

248   Gaspar, D F   *Apuntes de Apicultura*

-     1986   -   -   Spanish Good typescript.

A general manual of apiculture. 171 pps

10   -   FOR   -

---

249   Gay, John   *Fables*

| 92 | 1738 | - | - | Handsomely rebound. |

Fable X The Degenerate Bees. Author of 'The Beggar's Opera'. Book addressed to Dean Swift and believed to satirise Horace Walpole. Engraved plate of a skep hive by Gravelot and Scotin, with others.

| 50 | - | ANT |

250   Gayre, G R Lt.Col.   *Wassail! In Mazers of Mead*

| 643 | 1948 | - | 1st | Foxed, chipped dw Rare |

:an account of mead, metheglin ,sack and other ancient liquors and the mazer cups out of which they were drunk etc. Authoritative but its numerous scholarly classical references make it a less than entertaining read.

| 28 | - | 20thC |

251   Geary, H S   *The Beekeepers Vade Mecum*

| 489 | 1920 | - | Reprint | - |

A clever practical pocket reference book of its post-WW1 period. However for all its small format its suggests armchair and spectacles rather than a 'go with me' guide in one's bee-suit pocket.

| 20 | - | 20thC |

252   Geary, H S   *Another*

| 489 | 1920 | - | 1st | - | - |
| 25 | - | 20thC |

253   Geary, H S   *Bees for Profit & Pleasure*

| 447 | 1909 | - | 1st |

A handbook…with hints on the uses of honey and a beekeeper's calendar. "For ladies beekeeping is eminently suitable"

| 20 | - | OLD |

254   Geary, H S   *Another*

| 447 | 1909 | - | 1st | Fair. Damp stains |

A handbook, edited by Sanders. Makes an unusually early reference to Isle of Wight disease

| 10 | - | OLD |

255   Geary, H S   *Profitable Beekeeping*

| 542 | 1911 | - | 1st | Well- bound hb spine rubbed pages browned |

Thick paper and good photographs

| 40 | - | OLD |

256   Geary, H S   *Another*

| 452 | 1911 | 1919 | 4th |

Period photographs

| 20 | - | OLD | - |

257   Geary, H S   *Another*

| 452 | 1911 | 1919 | 4th |

Adverts for hives

| 20 | - | OLD |

258   Geary, H S   *Another*

452   1911   1923   5th New and revised   Limp copy. Slight tears to spine :

for smallholders and others. A less condescending title than works for cottagers of the 19th century. Makes further reference to Isle of Wight disease.

20   -   OLD

---

259   Gedde, John   *The English Apiary*

81   1721   -   -   Spine a mite loose..

: or the Complete Bee-master. "The principles laid down by Gedde and the hive he devised to carry them out entitle him to a high place in the roll of British Bee-masters" (Walker). He patented the hexagonal hive. Worlidge did not approve of it.

300   -   ANT

---

260   Gilman, A   *Practical bee-breeding*

644   1928   -   1st   T.Edwardes copy with critical letter 1929

Focuses on the potential benefits of bee breeding to achieve better stock by line-breeding or in-breeding. Proved somewhat contentious for Miss Betts.. The work of a practical man and an independent thinker.

60   -   20thC

---

261   Gilman, A   *Another*

644   1928   -   1st   -   -

30   -   20thC

---

262   Golding, Robert   *The Shilling Beebook*

256   1847   1847   1st   Limp copy. Repaired.

:containing the leading facts in the Natural History of Bees etc. "In spite of its low price…the work of a first-class beekeeper who influenced Bevan and helped in the preparation of his 'Honey Bee'…A dangerous rival to Huish" (Fraser). Dr Crane points out that Langstroth had a copy of this modest book with its description of 'an improved Grecian Hive' and that he lived in Kent near Charing where Wheler had lived in 1682. The idea of making side and bottom bars to rectangular frames, together with a bee-space all round them, was Langstroth's intuitive 'Eureka !' moment that revolutionised world beekeeping in 1851.

45   -   ANT

---

263   Goldsmith, O   *The Bee*

-   1759   1914   -   Classic. Oxford edition

Superb essays on interesting subjects. Nothing on bees except an essay on the sagacity of insects when he notes that a single bee is the most stupid insect imaginable, languishes for a while in solitude, and soon dies.

8   -   20thC

---

264   Graham-Smith, G & others   *Report on The Isle of Wight Disease*

456   1912   -   1st   Clean copy

Pub by HM Stationery Office for the Board of Agriculture. Has reports for 1912 and 1913. "Nosema apis is the agent responsible"

40   -   OLD

265 Green, W H B   *The Queen of the Golden Bees*

648a   1944   1944   1st   -

A fairy tale founded on fact for children.

15   -   20thC

---

266 Gregg, Dr A L   *The Philosophy & Practice of Beekeeping*

649   1949   -   1st   dw (2 copies)

Bee Craft book. Died 1981. He kept bees on his roof near Paddington Station. In Chapt. 12 he gives a bibliography with shrewd critical notes on 70 famous writers on bees and beekeeping.

15   2   20thC

---

267 Gregg, Dr A L   *Another*

649   1949   -   1st   hb (2 copies)   -

12   2   20thC

---

268 Gresham (Pub)   *The Structure of the Bee*

427   1903   -   1st   Pop-up model

An ingenious way of showing the structure of the bee in three dimensions. Made in cardboard with lifting flaps Queen and drone. Parts numbered and identified.

30   -   OLD

---

269 Gresham (Pub)   *Another*

427   1903   -   1st   Loose & rubbed. Pop-up model.   -

18   -   OLD

---

270 Gresham   *The Structure of the Bee*

427   1903   -   1st   -   -

18   -   OLD

---

271 H M S O   *Instruction in bee-keeping for the use of Irish bee-keepers*

432   1905   1912   -   New revised edition.

Excellent photographs for its period.

25   -   OLD

---

272 Hale, Thomas
A Compleat Body of Husbandry

108   1756   1756   1st   Bees pps255-261 A folio volume.

Front cover loose.

Hale' was possibly really Dr John Hill, an apothecary, quack doctor and prolific writer. He says the drone and queen are male and female and believes that wax is the faeces of the bees. (Fraser)

200   -   ANT

273 Hall, C A   *Bees, Wasps & Ants*

517   1925   1934   -   .

Peeps at Nature. Supposedly for children. 4 col plates and 8 b&w .Adopts a worthy learned style with sophisticated vocabulary.

10   -   20thC

---

274 Hall, C A   *Another*

517   1925   -   1st   dw chipped   -

10   -   20thC

---

275 Halleux   *Le Libre de Apiculteur Belge*

-            -   1911   -   Soft cover. Belgian in French

A manual with interesting early illustrations such as Kesel's diagonal hives.

35   -   FOR

---

276 Hamilton, William   *The Art of Beekeeping*

651   1945   1945   3rd imp. of 1s   (3 copies) 2nd and 3rd impressions of 1st.

Lecturer at W of Scot. Agric. College to 1920 then Leeds in 1926. Favours the WBC. An excellent manual. Clear and reliable.

8   3   20thC

---

277 Hamilton,William   *Another*

651   1945   1946   2nd   (2 copies)

8   2   20thC

---

278 Hamilton, William   *Another*

651   1945   1971   3rd   2nd impression. V clean copy.

8   -   20thC

---

279   .   -   ‒

---

280 Hansen, H   *Brood Diseases*

-            1987   -   1st   pb (2 copies)

Brilliant close-up colour plates to enable visual diagnosis of 8 brood afflictions

6   2   MOD

---

281 Hanssen, M   *Recipes with Honey*

-            1979   -   -   Small pamphlet

A little collection of recipes

2   -   MOD

---

282 Harker, Leonard   *Blazing the Trail*

652   1938   -   1st   Signed by Harker

: reminiscences of Dr. AZ Abushady- poet -bee-master - humanist. (1892-1955) of Egypt. He started the Apis Club in 1919 with Bee World as its magazine. This contribution in time led to the forming of the IBRA in 1949 under the leadership of Dr. Crane and the world centre for scientific information about bees. He experimented with artificial comb made of aluminium.

50	-	20thC

---

283   Harris, Moses   *The Aurelian*

-	1766	1986	1st reprint Mint large format

Natural history of English insects.;namely Moths and Butterflies together with the Plants on which they Feed. "The most splendid of all English entomological books" (Chalmers-Hunt).1730-1788 This magnificent reproduction by Country Life Books has a scholarly introduction by Robert Mays . The frontispiece is a self portrait of Harris and the large volume is rich with splendid coloured plates. Not about bees though.

25	-	ANT

---

284   Harris, W H   *The Honey Bee*

380	1884	-	1st	back cover and spine detached

:its nature ,homes and products. Religious Tract Society. Harris spoke to the BBKA on the educative influences of beekeeping in 1904. "The study of the honey-bee provides reason for…a sublime adoration of an infinite 'First Cause', I.e. the Deity" -but also a thorough and wide-ranging account of the whole subject

50	-	OLD

---

285   Harris, W H   *Another*

380	1884	-	1st	-	-
55	-	OLD			

---

286   Harris, W H   *Another*

380	1884	-	1st	Spine frayed	-
45	-	OLD			

---

287   Harrison, Charles   *The Book of the Honeybee*

425	j210	1903	1903	1st	Cover soiled

Handbook of Practical Gardening XIV Suggests cottagers save the £1 cost of a bar-hive by putting wooden supers on top of a skep. "The best hive is the WBC".

25	-	OLD

---

288   Harrison, Charles   *Another*

425	1903	1903	1st	Bright copy	-
25	-	OLD			

---

289   Harwood, A F   *British Bee Plants*

653	1947	-	1st	Paperback. Wadey's copy

Issued by the Apis Club. A solid and convenient account of bee pasturage.

10	-	20thC

---

290   Hasluck, Paul   *Beehives & Beekeepers Appliances*

431	1905	1912	-	-

Work Handbook Series. He was the editor of 'Work' , a journal giving technical details of all kinds of manufactured goods, machines and instruments. Precise details for craftsmen making appliances -WBC hives ,observation hives smokers, extractors etc as customary years ago. 'Practical, reliable, simply worded'

30   -   OLD   -

---

291   Hasluck, Paul   *Another*
431   1905   1907   -   Ex library. Well bound   -
36   -   OLD

---

292   Hawkins, K   *Beekeeping in the South*
J215   1920   1920   -

A Handbook on Seasons, Methods and Honey Flora of the Fifteen Southern States. An early rare work. Pub ABJ 10 adverts for books. Superb period photographs.

30   -   USA

---

293   Hawks, Ellison   *Bees Shown to the Children*
457   j218 1912   -   1st   -

Interesting coloured plates and photographs. Bee information on anatomy and behaviour; sound for intelligent children

10   -   OLD

---

294   Hawks,Ellison   *Another*
457   1912   -   1st   -   -
10   -   OLD

---

295   Hawks, E   *Another*
457   1912   -   1st   Faded. Small tears.
8   -   OLD

---

296   Hawks, E   *Another*
457   1912   -   1st   Loose pages
8   -   OLD

---

297   Hawks, E   *Another*
457   1912   -   1st   Scribbled. Coloured plate.
10   -   OLD

---

298   Hawks, E   *Another*
457   1912   -   1st   Bit rubbed
8   -   OLD

---

299   Hayes, G   *Nectar Producing Plants*
518   1925   -   1st   Limp. Spine rubbed

:and the pollen. An early remarkable attempt at drawings of pollen grains with advice on how to examine and record the findings. Pub BBJ

25   -   20thC

---

300   Heard, G   *A Taste for Honey*
656   USA 1941 1942   1st UK edition   Fair

A work of fiction. A novel with a bee-keeping theme.

10 · 20thC

---

301 Heath, Prof L   *A Case of Hives*

· 1985 · 1st   Back cover badly torn

Prof at Plymouth Univ. Died 2004. A compendium which 'subtly introduces new beekeepers to the irritation of selecting from the assortment of UK bee hives' (Glyn Davis) Appdx 1 is a useful explanation of beekeeping terms.

4 · MOD

302

· · · ·

---

303 Herrod-Hempsall, W   *Beekeeping Simplified*

471 1915 · 1st   Booklet

10 · OLD

---

304 Herrod-Hempsall, W
Beekeeping New and Old

658 1930/1937 · 1st   Vol 1 1930 & Vol 2

1937. Ex-library. Price for both volumes together.
:described with pen and camera. "The Doyen of British Beekeeping". He always advocated the WBC and deprecated alternatives. This book is "the more valuable because the publisher's plates were destroyed by German bombs near St Paul's Cathedral during the second World War" (Brown). Karl Showler regrets that this "vast collection of information...lack(s) any cohesion or effective indexing" A remarkable tour-de-force nevertheless. Vol 2 is scarce.

450 · 20thC

---

305 Herrod-Hempsall, W   *Another*

658 1930/1937 · 1st   Vol 1 1930 & Vol 2 1937. Vol 1 re-bound therefore not matching. Price for both volumes

together.

500 · 20thC

---

306 Herrod-Hempsall, W   *Beekeeping New and Old*

658 1930 · 1st   Vol 1 only. Small repairs. ·

75 · 20thC

---

307 Herrod-Hempsall, W   *Another*

658 1930 · 1st   Vol 1 only. Slightly loose. ·

60 · 20thC

---

308 Herrod-Hempsall,
W   *Producing, Preparing, Exhibiting and Judging Bee Produce*

458 1912 · 1st   Dedication by author to parents. Handwritten.

39

Pub by BBJ of which Herrod was joint-editor for 7 years and Secretary of the BBKA from 1909 to 1930. 168 pps. Preface by Cowan who says it 'supplies a long-felt want…by someone specially qualified for the task' Excellent period photographs.

| 40 | - | OLD |

---

309 Herrod-Hempsall, W
Producing, Preparing, Exhibiting and Judging Bee Produce

| 458 | 1912 | - | 1st | - | - |
| 20 | - | OLD |

---

310 Herrod-Hempsall, W   *Another*
| 458 | 1912 | 1912 | 1st | Bound. Gilt stamped. Signed 'Mollie from the author' | - |
| 25 | - | OLD |

---

311 Herrod-Hempsall, W   *Another*
| 458 | 1912 | 1912 | 1st | (3 Copies -limp-1 torn) | - |
| 15 | 3 | OLD |

---

312 Herrod-Hempsall, W   *Another*
| 458 | 1912 | 1948 | 2nd | Revised (2 copies) v clean |

Expanded version. 219 pps. With his brother, Joseph, he bought in 1925 from Cowan the BBJ. The brothers dominated British beekeeping until their deaths in 1951.

| 10 | - | OLD |

---

313 Herrod-Hempsall, W   *Another*
| 458 | 1912 | 1948 | 2nd | H Ashforth's copy | - |
| 15 | - | OLD |

---

314 -   ·

---

315 Herrod-Hempsall, W
Anatomy, physiology and natural history of the honey bee

| 659 | 1938 | 1943 | 2nd | (6 copies -1 with bare spine) |

400 illlustrations, photos by author. Pub by BBJ. 8 editions in all to 1947.Written in language devoid of jargon.

| 12 | 6 | 20thC |

---

316 -   ·

---

317 Herrod-Hempsall, W   *Another*
| 659 | 1938 | - | 1st |
| 15 | - | 20thC |

---

318 Herrod-Hempsall, W   *The Beekeepers Guide*
| 660 | 1938 | 1940 | 3rd | Larger limp cover. Wartime copy. |

:to the management of bees in moveable frame hives. 8 editions to 1947. Regularly recommended as an inexpensive novices guide book until well after WW2. Simple, sound and sane instruction.

| 4 | - | 20thC |

319   Herrod-Hempsall, W   *Another*

| 660 | 1938 | 1942 | 6th | Limp cover. Wartime copy. Slightly rubbed |
| 4 | - | 20thC | | |

320   Herrod-Hempsall, W   *Another*

| 660 | 1938 | 1942 | 5th | Limp cover. Wartime copy. |
| 4 | - | 20thC | | |

321   Herrod-Hempsall, W   *Another*

| 660 | 1938 | 1944 | 7th | Fine. Limp cover. Wartime copy. |
| 6 | - | 20thC | | |

322   Herrod-Hempsall, W   *Another*

| 660 | 1938 | 1947 | 8th | Limp cover loose on one of (2 copies) |
| 4 | 2 | 20thC | | |

323   Herzog   *The Swarm*

| 662 | 1974 | 1976 | - | pbs (2 copies) fair |

Book of the film. A horror story.

| 4 | 2 | MOD | | |

324   Hill, Thomas   *The Profitable Arte of Gardening*

| 7 | 1568 | 1586 | 7th | Black letter. Some writing |

Pub Robert Walde-grave. A remarkable book - the oldest in the collection. Hill translated, without acknowledgement, the Latin work of German physician Georgius Pictorius. Charles Butler grumbled about this but Pictorius is thought the best of the three encyclopaedias of the later 16th Century.

| 600 | - | ANT | | |

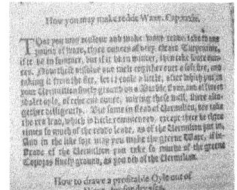

325   Hodges, D   *Pollen Loads of the Honeybee*

| 664 | 1952 | 1952 | 1st | - |

:a guide to the identification by colour and form. Contains a chart of pollen load colours recorded in the South of England. Pub BRA. 6 charts of hand-mounted colours. " Nearly 200 individual pollen grains carefully drawn to scale. Each of the 350 paper slips was cut from large sheets of hand-painted colour, giving 14mm squares which were individually pasted in" (Brown) A classic work of art and study. 1898-1979.

| 190 | - | 20thC | | |

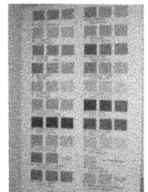

326   Hodges, D   *Another*

| 664 | 1952 | 1952 | 1st | - |
| 190 | - | 20thC | | |

327   Hodges, D   *Another*

| 664 | 1952 | 1974 | - | Facsimile edition. |
| 40 | - | 20thC | | |

328a Hodgkinson, R   *The Farmer Needs Bees*

| - | No date | - | - | 10 page pamphlet |

A succinct paper advocating bees as vital pollinators for fruit and seeds

| 2 | - | MISC |

328b Hodgson, Natalie B   *Childrens' Books on Bees and Beekeeping*

| - | 1973 | - | Reprint BRA | Large format   limp |

5 pps 346 titles listed, 271 in English

| 20 | - | BAB |

---

330 Hommell, R *Apiculture*

| - | 1919 | 1919 | 3rd | French. Revised Limp uncut |

Professor Regional d'Apiculture. Good period Gallic illustrations

| 50 | - | FOR |

---

331 Hooper & Morse *Illustrated Enclopedia of Beekeeping*

| - | 1985 | - | 1st | Signed by Hooper. dw |

The definitive modern resource. Comprehensive, authoritative and global in scope by the most renowned practical experts in the UK and USA. 45 exponents contributed to the entries.

| 30 | - | MOD |

---

332 Hooper & Taylor *The Beekeepers Garden*

| - | 1988 | - | 1st | - |

A comprehensive guide to making a bee-garden and the selection and cultivation of appropriate plants. Colour photographs.

| 15 | - | MOD |

---

333 Hooper, M M *Common Sense Beekeeping*

| 667 | 1939 | no date | - | Poor. Limp |

Pub by Link House. Miss Hooper was one of only three inter-war lady bee authors. She favoured the 'Glamorgan Method of Bee Management' and encouraged the "let-alone methods of beekeeping popular in the 1950's"(Showler). Her book justifies its title and was favourably reviewed by Annie Betts.

| 5 | - | 20thC |

---

334 Hooper, M M *Another*

| 667 | 1939 | no date | - | - |

| 4 | - | 20 |

---

335 Hooper, M M *Another*

| 667 | 1939 | 1946 | 3rd | - |

| 10 | - | 20thC |

---

336 Hooper, M M *Another*

| 667 | 1939 | 1946 | 3rd | - |

| 12 | - | 20thC |

---

337 Hooper, Ted   *Guide to Bees & Honey*

668   1976   -   1st   (3 copies) dws

WE (Ted) Hooper was County Beekeeping Lecturer at Writtle Agric Coll, Essex. "One of the most useful and popular books of recent times" (Stevens). Reckoned the standard textbook for UK beekeepers in the last quarter of the 20th century

13   -   MOD

338 Hooper, Ted   *Another*

668   1976   1983   2d revised dw

Includes oilseed rape

13   3   MOD

339 Hopkins, I H   *42 Years Beekeeping in New Zealand*

519a   1916?   -   -   -

"IHH was for several years NZ Govt Apiarist ,and the flourishing state of beekeeping in that country is mainly due to his untiring energy and power of organisation" (Walker) Together with the book is a long personal letter to Tickner Edwardes dated 1917 and Regulations re the export of honey taken from the NZ Gazette.

40   -   OLD

340 Houghton, W   *Sketches of British Insects*

-        -   1877   2nd   Coloured plates & wood engravings

Little on bees. Very fine plates and wood engravings.

40   -   OLD

341 Howe, R & W   *Practical Beekeeping*

-        1980   -   1st   (3 copies-2 green,1 blue)

A handsome hardbacked book for beginners - beekeeping simply explained

15   3   MOD

342 Howes, FN *Plants & Beekeeping*

670   1945   1945   1st   (8 copies)

:an account of those plants ,wild and cultivated, of value to the hive bee etc. Recognised as the standard work on the subject. 32 photographs.

15   8   20thC

343 Howes, FN *Another*

670   1945   1979   2nd   pb (4 copies)

No photos except on covers. Reissued with an entry by Dr Free on oilseed rape and a supplementary bibliography by Dr Crane

8   4   20thC

344 Howes, FN
**   *A Dictionary of Useful and Everyday Plants and their Common Names***

-        1974   1975   dw mint Reprint with corrections

Dr Howes died 1973 shortly after completing his typescript. He was formerly Keeper of the Museum, Royal Botanic Gardens, Kew.

20   -   20thC

345   Hoyt, M   *The World of Bees*

671 j236 1965US   1966   1st UK   -

An enthusiast with a friendly conversational style, but incidentally very informative.

10   -   20ᵗʰC

---

346   Huber, Francis   *New Observations*

171   1806   -   1841   -

1750-1831 The first proper entomological description of the life history of the honey bee. His work was 'the subject of sharp controversy in many lands' (Fraser) Translated by Sir JG Dalzell from the French original of 1792. Being blind he relied on his manservant, Francis Burnens, to record his work. He invented the leaf hive which gave ready access to combs and demonstrated the real source of beeswax.

150   -   ANT

---

347   Huber, Francis   *Another*

171   1806   -   1st   -

Anderson, Edinburgh

250   -   ANT

---

348   Huber, Francis   *Another*

171   1806   -   1st   lacks illustrations

200   -   ANT

---

349   Huber, Francis   *Another*

171   1806   1808   2nd   original boards uncut

200   -   ANT

---

350   Huber, Francis   *Another*

171   1806   1808   2nd   -

Flyleaves have an article from ABJ of 1946 pasted in

200   -   ANT

---

351   Huber, Francis   *Another*

171   1806   1808   2nd   a little foxed. Back cover detached

200   -   ANT

---

352   Huber, Francis   *Another*

171   1806   1841   v good condition

150   -   ANT

---

353   Huber, Francis   *Another*

171 J238 1806   -   1926   Handsome volumes

Dadant's fullest version

35   -   ANT

---

354 Huber, Francis *Another*

171 J238 1806 - 1926

35 - ANT

---

355 Huber, Francis *Another*

171 J238 1806 - 1926 Inscribed

35 - ANT

---

356 Huish, Robert
A Treatise on the nature, economy and practical management of bees

176 1815 1844 - -

Portrait of Huish. He died 1850. Describes the lives of foreign apiarians. Attacked "the absurdities of Mr Huber". A skeppist who disapproved of hives that could be looked into.

120 - ANT

---

357 Huish, Robert *A Treatise On Bees*

176 1815 - 1st a little foxed. Uncut. rebound

300 - ANT

---

358 Huish, Robert *Another*

176 1815 1817 2nd Handsomely rebound.

300 - ANT

---

359 Huish, Robert *Another*

176 1815 1817 2nd a nice copy

300 - ANT

---

360 Huish, Robert *Instructions for Using...*

183 1819 1980 - Reprint

Northern Bee Books 24 pps. Instructions for using the Huish Hive. Combs extracted without killing bees.

15 - ANT

---

361 Huish, Robert *The Cottager's Manual*

184 1820 1821 2nd Printed covers

The suffocating and depriving systems and how to buy hives and manage them. Has 5 pps of advertisements for religious books.

150 - ANT

---

362 Hunter, John *A Manual of Beekeeping*

333 1875 1876 - Reprint of 2nd edition

Hon.Sec. of BBKA. His manual "almost became the official book of the period"(Stevens). Written to provide a 'moderately priced' book on how to cope with bees.

60 - OLD

---

363   Hunter, John   *Another*

333   1875   1879   3rd   Revised edition

36 pps of adverts for books and equipment

60   -   OLD

---

364   Hunter, John   *Another*

333   1875   1879   3rd   -

60   -   OLD

---

365   Hunter, John   *Another*

333   1875   1884   4th   -

55   -   OLD

---

366   Hutchinson, W Z   *Advanced Bee Culture: Its Methods and Management*

J231   1891   1918   5th   Book plate

Pub Root A Michigan commercial beekeeper, writing for other professionals and drawing on the best that has appeared in The Beekeepers' Review' which he edited and his own experience sets out what is needed in managing bees for profit. This copy was Miss Cummings' 5th prize for honey in 1923. Magnificent pastoral photoplates, including a 700 colony apiary in N.Y.

40   -   USA

---

367   Hutchinson, W Z   *The Production of Comb Honey*

J240   1887   1887   1st   Small limp

An early US work. 22 pps of wonderful old advertisements for supplies and appliances. He then recommended using 'starters' only in the brood nest when hiving swarms.

20   -   USA

---

368   Hyde, G   *Teach Yourself Entomology*

-      1961   -   1st   -

Teach Yourself Series (EUP) Bees pps 43-61

8   -   MISC

---

369   I T P   *Candle Manufacture*

-      -   -   -   Small pamphlet

Intermediate Technology Publications 19 pps on simple techniques

2   -   MOD

370a IBRA *Garden Plants Valuable to Bees*

-      1981   -   1st   pb

52 pps listing plants with their Botanical and Common names, descriptions and, by use of N and P, flowers visited for nectar and pollen collection. Preface by Dr Crane.

8   -   MOD

370b **IBRA** *Bee World*

| - | - | - | - | Magazines |

7 copies sold as one lot.1991 and 1980

| 7 | - | MOD |

---

371 **Imms,Dr. AD** *Insect Natural History*

| - | 1947 | 1947 | 1st | Bees p271-273 |

Many superb coloured plates. Downing College Cambridge, Reader in Entomology. Scholarly work.

| 20 | - | MISC |

---

372 **Imms,Dr. AD** *Another*

| - | 1947 | 1947 | 1st | Faded spine |

| 20 | - | MISC |

---

373 **Imms,Dr. AD** *Outlines of Entomology*

| - | 1942 | 1944 | 2nd | Revised |

96 illustrations. An introduction to basic principles. Many references to the hive bee

| 20 | - | MISC |

---

374 **Ioyrish, N** *Bees & People*

| - | 1974 | - | 1st | |

| 15 | - | 20thC |

---

375 **Ioyrish, N** *Another*

| - | 1977 | - | - | dw |

Translated from Russian by GA Kozlova. A comprehensive survey celebrating honey for healthy living with interesting recipes for food and drink. The bibliography records Russian contributors to the progress of beekeeping while recognising Western beemasters. Claims that Prokopovich(1775-1850) invented the important 'collapsible hive', promoted bee farming and used wooden frames to give access to combs.

| 15 | - | 20thC |

---

376 **Ipsen,D C** *What Does a Bee See?*

| - | 1971 | - | 1st | dw |

Interesting coloured photographs. Concerned with methods of scientific research as well as the question in the title.

| 12 | - | USA |

---

377 **Ireland Dept. of Agriculture** *Irish Beekeepers Manual*

| 677 | 1958 | 1958 | 1st | Limp copy,slight tear to spine |

The successor to Instruction In Beekeeping of 1905 IBRA No 432 Contains hive plans.

| 15 | - | 20thC |

---

378 - -

---

379   Isecht, Jane   *Honeybees*

-	1973	-	1st	For children
15	-	USA		

---

380   Jackson, I H   ***Beekeeping for Beginners***

510	1924	-	1st	8 plates - 1 coloured

Pub Blackie. Miss Ivy Jackson was one of the few ladies in print in this era.(died 1932). Illustrated with period plates, microscopic photographs and line drawings. Simple, straightforward language style

12	-	20thC		

---

381   Jackson, I H   ***Another***

510	1924	-	1st	-
12	-	20thC		

---

382   Jackson, I H   ***Another***

510	-	1945	-	Reprints with index. (5 copies- 3 with dws)-
8	5	20thC		

---

383   James, E L B   ***Beekeeping for Beginners and Others***

678	1950	1950	1st	(4 copies -2 with dws)

41 plates. Major James was a hobbyist who became a commercial beekeeper, queen rearer and contributor to the BBJ. Homely photos and illustrations of equipment courtesy of the manufacturers. Very well-informed and reader-friendly with anecdotes of beekeeping while he was stationed in Egypt and writing the book in a tent.

12	4	20thC		

---

384   James, Rev Thomas   ***The Honeybee***

239	1842	1852	Reprint	Bound with 570 & a book on gardening and a book on soils

"Reading for the rail" or entertaining reading! Draws on all the celebrated authors. Reprinted from the 'Quarterly Review'.

160	-	ANT		

---

385   Jenyns, Rev C F G
A Book About Bees

390	1886	1886	1st

:their history ,habits and instincts…for young readers. Introduction by the President of BBKA. Steel engravings of a 'bee tent'and a cottager shifting bees from a skep to a moveable frame hive. Older and very literate young readers must have been the target audience. "Intelligent boys and girls will find a hive or two of bees quite within their powers of management".

50	-	OLD

---

386   Jenyns, Rev C F G   *Another*

390	1886	1886	1st	Joints slightly loose
45	-	OLD		

387   Johansson,TSK and MP   *Apicultural Literature Published in Canada and The United States*

-       1972   1972   1st   Duplicated typescript

Bibliography based on 10 major libraries. Frequently referred to in this catalogue by j and a number.

15   -   BAB

---

388   Johansson,TSK and MP   *Some Important Operations in Bee Management*

-       1978   -   1st   pb (2 copies)

Togi died 2001. Valuable articles on best practice in beekeeping-handling feeding, queen-rearing etc. collected from Bee World. Foreword by Dr Crane

8   2   MOD

---

389   Johnstone (Mrs)
Scenes of Industry displayed by the beehive and the ant-hill

203   1827   1830   2nd   Nicely re-bound

A childrens' instructional book told by dialogue between Letitia and a knowledgeable beekeeper,including a story of a man who charms bees into following him by keeping a queen in his ear. 6 famous plates.

100   -   ANT

---

390   Johnstone (Mrs)   *Scenes of Industry*

203   1827   -   1st   Fragile spine. Fine plates

100   -   ANT

---

391   Jones & Jones   *Y gwenynydd*

399   1888   -   1st   Welsh book

Welch language. Claimed by the authors to be the first such book. Adverts in both languages for appliances and Cowan's books.

100   -   OLD

---

392   Jones, Bridget   *Gales Honey Book*

-       1983   -   1st   -

Modern recipes and the story of Gales Honey, founded at Mortlake and now(1973) at Norwich

8   2   MOD

---

393 Kelley, Walter T *Queen Breeding*

J259   nd   ·   ·   Duplicated reprint 20 pages

of Paducah,Kentucky. Invented a plastic super A concise little guide booklet with handwritten cover.

10   ·   USA

394a Kelsey, W E *The Spell of the Honeybee*

682   1945   ·   1st   (5 copies-2 with dw)

The introduction includes an analysis of the various genres of beekeeping books. It is both a manual of practice and a pleasurable read at the fireside. Contemplative but accurate, well illustrated,scientific and keen on home construction of equipment.

12   5   20thC

394b Kelsey, W E *The Spell of the Honeybee*

682   1945   1947   2nd revised   (2 copies-1 with dw)

12   2   20thC

395 Kennedy-Bell, M G   *The Joys of Beekeeping*

562   1932   ·   1st   (2 copies)

Miss Bell gave a course of lectures for the BBC. A simply-phrased encouraging book for beginners.

30   2   20thC

396 Kennedy-Bell, M G   *Another*

562   1932   ·   1st   Loose pages

15   ·   20thC

397 Keys, John *The Practical Bee Master*

135   1780   ·   1st   Covers detached.

Straw hives and boxes. Managing bees without killing them with "occasional strictures on Mr Thomas Wildman's "Treatise on Bees". Used metal dividing plates between 'storyfied' boxes on skeps.

320   ·   ANT

398 Keys, John *The Antient Bee Masters Farewell*

154   1796   ·   1st   Uncut. Original boards.

"Double and treble hives or boxes with remarks on Schirach and others". Denies Schriach's discovery that a queen could be reared from a worker larva. The title means not an old beekeepers goodbye, but an experienced expert's way to manage things properly.

350   ·   ANT

399 Keys, John *Another*

154   1796   ·   1st   Rebound. Spine slightly bumped.

450   ·   ANT

400a Keys, John *Another*

154   1796   ·   1st   Rebound

450   ·   ANT

400b Keys, John *Another*

154	1796	-	1st	Nice clean copy
350	-	ANT		

401 Keys, John *Another*

154	1796	1814	-	-
300	-	ANT		

402 Khalifman, I *Bees*

-	1951	1953	1st Eng	(3 copies)

Russian. Stalin Prize. English edition. He says our views on bee life and organisation reflect our political ideologies. Notes with regret that bees unlike other life forms have not been changed in characteristics by selective breeding under domestic conditions. Deprecates' the law of the jungle' in nature and looks to 'the harmony and cooperation of a species' to inform Soviet progess.[? reflecting Marx's theory of alienation and the goodwill of the proletariat]. A remarkable book for all that.

10	3	20thC

403 Kirby, Rev William *Monographia apum Angliae*

165	1802	-	1st	2 handsomely bound volumes. Uncut

An attempt to divide into their natural genera and families such species of the Linnean genus Apis as have been discovered in England. Ipswich Printed for the author by J Raw, Fleet Street. 14 and 18 plates in 2 volumes. 300 species listed

450	-	ANT

404 Laidlaw & Eckert *Queen Rearing*

-	1950	1950	1st	-

Important American researchers in bee genetics and artificial insemination. Univ. of California at Davis. Chap 1 gives a sound account of the history of queen rearing, mainly in the USA.

20	-	USA

405 Laidlaw, Harry H *Contemporary Queen Rearing*

-	1979	1979	1st	Near mint

Pub Dadant. "I have stood on the shoulders of giants" - Laidlaw quoting Sir Isaac Newton about the 10 close-packed pages of references to authors who had contributed to his study and understanding.

20	-	USA

406 Laidlaw, Harry H *Another*

-	1978	1978	1st	-
20	-	USA		

407 Laidlaw, Harry H *Instrumental Insemination of Honey Bee Queens*

-	1977	-	1st	Ring binding

Short texts but brilliant close-up photographs

15	-	USA

408 Langstroth, Lorenzo L *Hive and Honeybee*
J284   1853   1919   20th   Signed by Arthur M Sturges.Cover slightly loose.
First revised by Dadant (see No 177) "A description of the most successful moveable-frame hive that had ever been invented" (Laidlaw) "Good literature as well as good beekeeping" (Comstock).
35   -   USA

409 Langstroth, Lorenzo L *Another*
J284   -   1977   -   Mint
Root reprint. "This masterpiece of beekeeping literature" (John A Root in his Preface)
30   -   USA

410 Langstroth (Grout)   *Langstroth on the Hive & the Honeybee*
-    1946   1946   1st   Revised edition
Updated by Dadant "One book that no beekeeper can afford to be without" (ABJ)
20   -   USA

411 Lardner, D *The Bee and White Ants*
287   1856   1856   1st   Rare
:their manners and habits. With illustrations of animal instinct and intelligence. A collection of periodicals issued in penny numbers.
50   -   OLD

412 Latter, O H *Bees and Wasps*
462   1913   1913   1st
Cambridge Manuals of Science and Literature. Senior science master at Charterhouse and formerly tutor of Keble Coll,Oxford. Short bibliog. of sources.
20   -   OLD

413 Latter, O H *Another*
462   1913   1913   1st   -
20   -   OLD

414 Latter, O H *Another*
462   1913   1913   1st   (2 copies)
20   2   OLD

415 Laurence, Rev John   *A New System of Agriculture*
83   1726   1726   1st   Folio volume. Front cover loose. Bees pps 154-161
One of the earliest of the many 'Reverent Gentlemen' who have made their numerous contributions to the bee literature.
200   -   ANT

416   Lawes, Geoff   *The Bee Book Book*
-          1991   -   1st   Mint pb (8 copies)
An extensively illustrated guide to the language and practice of collecting books
about bees. Pub NBB.
9   8   BAB

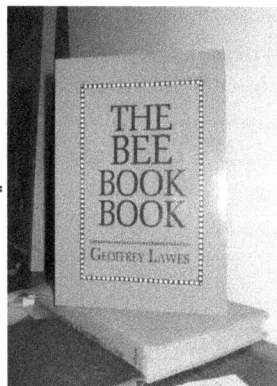

THE
BEE
BOOK
BOOK
GEOFFREY LAWES

417   Lawes, Geoff   *Another*
-          1991   -   1st   Mint hb (3 copies) in cases
A work by the vendor, being an introduction and guide for collectors of
books,with particular reference to bee subjects.
16   3   BAB

418   Lawson, J W*Honeycraft :in theory and practice*
688   1931   1948   3rd revised   (2 copies)
An excellent concise and informative book of its period
15   2   20thC

419   Lawson, J W   *Another*
688   1931   -   1st   -
20   20thC

420   Lawson, William
         A New Orchard and Garden with the Country Housewife's Garden
20   1618   1631   -   Beautifully   rebound
Bees pps 98-106   A Yorkshire gardener who advocated high conical straw hives under a penthouse roof beside a
warm orchard wall. The water used to drown the bees good for making mead.
210   -   ANT

421
-          -

422   Lawson, William   *Another*
20   1618   1683   -   Handsomely rebound.
with a woodcut of skeps in 'frame' or penthouse. Bees pps 75-81
150   -   ANT

423   Lawson, William   *The Country Housewife's Garden*
20   1618   1983   Reprint   dw
:together with The Husbandry of Bees and selections from New Orchard and Garden. Country Classics
20   -   ANT

424   Lecht, J   *Honeybees*
-          1973   -   1st   Large format
For young children. Superb pictures. 32 pps.
10   -   USA

425 Leeming, J F   *Claudius the Bee*

| 689 | 1936 | - | 1st | Very clean copy |

| 25 | - | 20thC |

---

426 Leeming, J F   *Another*

| 689 | 1936 | 1936 | Oct'36 | Reprint of 1st |

For children. "The story line is more important than the beekeeping or any natural history…very readable" (Showler)

| 15 | - | 20thC |

---

427 Leeming, J F   *Another*

| 689 | 1936 | 1980 | - | Fine. 3rd issue | - |

| 15 | - | 20thC |

---

428 Leeming, J F   *Another*

| 689 | 1936 | 1936 | 1st | - | - |

| 15 | - | 20thC |

---

429 Leeming, J F   *Thanks to Claudius*

| 689a | 1937 | - | 1st | - |

A sequel to 425. "Never so good as the story that preceded it" (Author's Preface)

| 15 | - | 20thC |

---

430 Lepper, F   *The Bees (A Play)*

| - | 1967 | - | - | Rare. Ex printer's library |

An unusual collectors' item. An odd,donnish,esoteric play. The hive is a metaphor for an Oxford college. Author's publication. Many historical notes and 70 tips at the end.

| 25 | - | MOD |

---

431 Leuenberger,Dr Fritz   *Les Abeilles*

| - | 1929 | - | - | uncut In French from |

German
Scientific. Anatomy and Physiology.

| 40 | - | FOR |

---

432 Lewellen, J B   *The Junior True Book of Honeybees*

| 691 J292 | 1958 | 1953 | 1962 | 3rd Imp |

For children aged 8 to 10 years

| 12 | - | 20thC |

433   Liger, le Sieur   *Oeconomie Generale de la Campagne ou Nouvelle Maison Rustique*   -   -   1701   Rev and corrected   Cover slightly loose.French Large

A magnificent old book. The origin of this work was 'Praedium Rusticum',a collection of tracts on agriculture compiled by Ch. Estienne (Stevens), Dr of Medicine in Paris and published after his death by Jean Libault in 1564 (Walker) Vols 1 and 2 together.

375   -   FOR

434

---

435   Lisney, Amy   *The Bee Walk*
694   1953   -   1st   dw. Published by author

:being the romance and practice of beekeeping. Mrs Lisney was from Dublin -the only Irish woman's book. Dedicated to her younger son Vernon killed in Burma 1943. 21 photos and illustrations. "Very readable and enjoyable" (Showler)

15   -   20thC

---

436   Longford, H   *The Castle that Hung in the Air*
695   1946   -   1st

Fanciful with fairies and an anthropomorphic bee written for the author's grandchildren

15   -   20thC

---

437   Lovell, J A   *The Flower & the Bee*
485 j308 1918   1920   -   Uncut

plant life and pollination.119 illustrations. A study of US plants.

40   -   OLD

---

438   Lovell, J A   *Another*
485   1918   1920   -   "   -

40   -   OLD

---

439   Lubbock, John   *On the Origin and Metamorphoses of Insects*
329   1873   1895   5th   Fine.

Baron Avebury MP,FRS.DCL,Ll D. Macmillan's Nature Series. A scholarly work First President of BBKA 1874-78.

20   -   OLD

---

440   Lubbock, John   *Ants, Bees & Wasps*
366   1882   -   2nd   -

:a record of observations …of the social hymenoptera. Lubbock found ants more convenient than bees. (IBRA) Fewer stings? A disciple of Darwin.

20   -   OLD

---

441   Lubbock, John   *Another*
366   1882   1915   Rev 3rd imp of 17th -

Vice-Chancellor, Univ of London

20   -   OLD

---

442 Lubbock, John   *Observations on Bees & Wasps*

366   1870's   -   -   3 pamphlets, unbound in a case

Ants, Imperial Policy and Observations on Bees and Wasps (from Linnean Society's Journal)

30   -   OLD

---

443 Lund, H J   *A Man & His Bees*

696   1947   -   1st   dw

:a beekeeper's chronicle. An indulgence for lovers of country ways. Includes tributes to Reaumur, Huber and Cobbett.

15   -   20ᵗʰC

---

444 Lundgren, Alexander   *Larobok I Biskotsel*

-      1922   1943   6th   Swedish

A general manual with appropriate illustrations

10   -   FOR

---

445 Mace, Herbert   *The Complete Handbook of Beekeeping*

706   1976   -   1st   (4 copies- 1 with missing flyleaf page)

Prepared by Owen Meyer. Expanded title of 447. Sound advice and a wealth of knowledge. Over 80 photographs and line drawings

20   4   20ᵗʰC

---

446 Mace,Herbert   *Another*

706   1976   -   Revised & reprinted

15   -   20ᵗʰC

---

447 Mace,Herbert   *The Beekeeper's Handbook*

706   1952   -   -   -

The original version. Finishes with a list of valuable beekeeping literature with dates. Well illustrated.

25   -   20ᵗʰC

---

448 Mace,Herbert   *Another*

706   1952   -   1st   Spine sunned

20   -   20ᵗʰC

---

449 Mace,Herbert   *Practical Beekeeping*

-      1977   -   -   (3 copies) pb mint

Mace's last work.Edited in consultation with Karl Showler

10   3   20ᵗʰC

---

450 Mace, H   *Adventures Among Bees*

505   1923   -   -   { 5 copies)

"amusing about his early experiences…will strike a familiar chord" (Dodd) Acarine problems! 17 photoplates

10   5   20ᵗʰC

---

451 Mace, H   *Another Bee Matters and Bee Masters*

701   1930   -   -   pb Frontispiece missing

with an appendix 'Who's Who in Beekeeping' May have upset people he omitted. His own entry concludes "Expelled from BBKA by Council, 1929"

10   -   20thC

---

452 Mace, H   *Another*

701   1930   1944   2nd   Orange Cover. Water-stained at margins

Frontispiece of Edwardes and Betts

10   -   20thC

---

453 Mace, H   *Another*

701   1930   1944   2nd   Clean copy. Many portraits

10   -   20thC

---

454 Mace, H   *A Book About the Bee*

493   1921   -   -   (3 copies)

Mace's first book. 22 photoplates. He spent three years in the Balkans in WW1 returning with malarial fever to find his holding built over. He evolved as a lecturer,experimenter and popular writer. He was the first to show beekeeping on TV in 1937. He designed a hive scale,tool box and concrete stand.

10   3   20thC

---

455 Mace, H   *Beefarming in Britain*

702   1936   -   -   hb scarce

Pub The Beekeeping Annual. Principal bee books listed.

10   -   20thC

---

456 Mace, H   *Another*

702   1936   -   -   Limp . Covers loose and foxed

10   -   20thC

---

457 Mace, H   *Some Other Bees, Butterflies and Moths*

520   1925   -   -   (3 copies- 1 split)

A collection of essays. Bees pps11-40 14 plates

10   3   20thC

---

458 Mace, H   *Bees, Flowers & Fruit*

705   1949   1949   1st   dw

:the story of insect-plant relations, flower structures and pollination described

10   -   20thC

Geoffrey Lawes

459 Mace, H *Modern Beekeeping*
699 1927 - 1st (Special) Author's gift to
Tickner Edwardes. Signed photograph of author Begins with a
'Sermon' addressed to Brother Beekeepers,pontificating
on I o W disease, frame size etc.The manual is in four
sections. This a Personal Edition and has 16 page plates
and over 100 other period illustrations. A special copy, one
of only 200 printed.
50 - 20ᵗʰC

460 Mace, H *Another*
699 1927 1933 Revised -
The sermon has become a Preface. He is now advocating
single-walled hives in preference to WBCs. This book cost
five shillings, a full day's wages then
10 2 20ᵗʰC

461
-

- - -

462 Mace, H *Beeswax*
704a 1930 - - (2 copies) Rare pamphlets
8 2 20ᵗʰC

463 Mace, H *Bee Gardens*
704 1944 - - Pamphlet - rare
8 - 20ᵗʰC

464 Mace, H *Beehives*
- 1944 - - Pamphlet - rare
and Bee Houses by John Spiller.
8 - 20ᵗʰC

465 Mace, H *The Beekeeping Annual 1930*
- 1930 - 1st Paperback
Mace edited the Annual for several years. This one has a review of Walker's 1929 catalogue and lists
experts,traders,associations etc.
8 - 20ᵗʰC

466 Maeterlinck, M *The Life of the White Ant*
- - 1927 2nd imp dw
Work by the celebrated Belgian Author
10 - MISC

467 **Maeterlinck, M** *The Life of the Bee*

422   1901   1912   -   -

Translated by Alfred Sutro from La vie des abeilles of 1901. The most celebrated work of literature based on bees.

15   -   OLD

---

468 **Maeterlinck, M** *Another*

422   1901   1912   -   28cm book

13 coloured plates by Edward J Detmold, an accomplished and respected artist

100   -   OLD

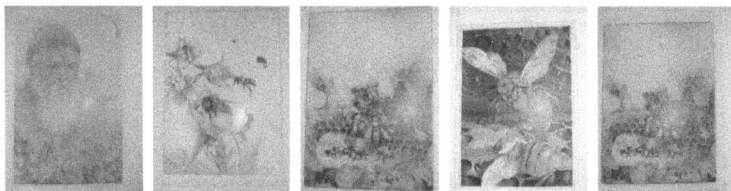

---

469 **Maeterlinck, M** *Another*

422   1901   1912   -   13 Detmold plates

An "exquisite piece of literature and social philosophy...the Homer of the bees" (Comstock)

100   -   OLD

---

470 **Maeterlinck, M** *Another*

422   1901   1909   -   Pocket edition

5   -   OLD

---

471 **Maeterlinck, M** *Another*

422   1901   no date   -   Pocket edition

8   -   OLD

---

472 **Maeterlinck, M** *Another*

422   1901   no date   -   Pocket edition

5   -   OLD

---

473 **Maeterlinck, M** *Another*

422   1901   -   1st   -

15   -   OLD

---

474 **Maeterlinck, M** *Another*

422   1901   1901   reprint of 1st   Trans Sutro

15   -   OLD

---

475 **Maeterlinck, M** *Another*

422   1901   1911   -   (2 copies)

10   2   OLD

---

476 Maeterlinck, M   *Another*

422	1901	1911	reprint	1st rubbed uncut, foxed, bibliog. In appdx
10	-	OLD		

---

477 Maeterlinck, M   *The Children's Life of the Bee*

490	j323	1920	US1919	1934	-	Bound with another + Queen Bomba etc

"He was a man who shrank from society,and spent much of his time in a world of conjecture and dreams"(Dodd).
The mating of the queen suitably bowdlerised!

| 25 | - | 20ᵗʰC | |

---

478 Maeterlinck, M   *Les Tresor des Humbles*

422a	1896	-	-	French

The Belgian master strikes again.

| 20 | - | FOR | |

---

479 Manley, R O B   *Honey Production in the British Isles*

713	1936	1936	1st	Spine rubbed

1887-1977. His 90 years life work was dedicated to making commercial beekeeping pay. He first identifies two types
of wax moth.. Pub Bradley. 15 plates

| 20 | - | 20ᵗʰC | |

---

480 Manley, R O B   *Another*

713	1936	1848	3rd imp	(2 copies- 1 with dw)

Faber &Faber recognise a classic author 25 photos. "His books are still highly regarded" (Brown)

| 20 | 2 | 20ᵗʰC | |

481a Manley, R O B   *Honey Farming*

714	1946	1946	1st	Various conditions some with fading but all good.(7 copies)

Numerous photographs mainly by CP Abbott

| 25 | 7 | 20ᵗʰC | |

481b Manley, R O B   *Another*

714	1946	1948	3rd imp	-
25	-	20ᵗʰC		

---

482 Manley, R O B   *Another*

714	1946	1949	4th imp	
25	-	20ᵗʰC		

---

483 Manley, R O B   *Beekeeping in Britain*

715	1948	1948	1st	Chipped dw

Many photos by Abbott,Rowse and others. 4 coloured. "It is impossible not to enjoy his company" (Dodd) After
Manley's son John died in 1976 the family bequeathed 462 books to the IBRA which ROB had collected

| 25 | - | 20ᵗʰC | |

---

484   Manley, R O B   *Another*

715	1948	1948	1st
25	-	20ᵗʰC	

485   Manley, R O B   *Another*

715	1948	1948	1st	Rebound in green cloth by Boots Library
30	-	20ᵗʰC		

486   Manley, R O B   *Another*

715	1948	1948	1st	Spine soiled
20	-	20ᵗʰC		

487   Manley, R O B   *Another*

715	1948	1948	1st	-
20	-	20ᵗʰC		

488   Manley, R O B   *Another*

715	1948	1948	1st	-
20	-	20ᵗʰC		

489a Markham, Gervase   *The Whole Art of Husbandry*

9	1614	1631	5th	Uncut Some worm holes and damaged spine.

:contained in four books now Renewed,corrected,enlarged and adorned with all the experiments and practices of our English Nation which were wanting in the Former Editions. First written by Conrade Heresbatch and translated by Barnaby Googe. Black letter typescript. Written in dialogue form. Bee matter (pps 355-385) follows Virgil and Columella. Markham was a prolific writer on agriculture, horsemanship etc. Straw or wicker hives recommended "A talented man with the kind of insatiable curiosity characteristic of the founders of the Royal Society later in the 17th Century" (FNL Poynter-quoted in IBRA)

150	-	ANT

489b Markham, Gervase   *Husbandman's Recreations*

9	-	? 1684	-	lacks covers

Bees pps 138-141 Text similar to 489c.Part of a volume 'A Way to get Wealth' combining this book with Lawson' s 'New Orchard' in all likelihood.

200	-	ANT

489c Markham, Gervase   *Cheap and Good Husbandry*

19	-	1683	14th impression	Clean Nicely rebound

:for the well-Ordering of all Beafts and Fowls Printed by T.B. for Hannah Sawbridge. Inscribed p145 'Bookish..Look at me you dog'

250	-	ANT

489d Markham, Gervase   *Farewell to Husbandry*

-	-	1684	-	lacks covers

No bees treated here. 'Farewell' means manage profitably,not 'goodbye'.

150	-	ANT

490 Markham, Gervase   *Cheape and Good Husbandry*

19   1614   1631   5th   lacks covers

:for the well ordering of beasts and fowls. Part of a larger volume. Printed by Nicholas Okes for John Harrison. Bees pps 177-182

200   -   ANT

491 Mayne, W   *A Swarm in May*

717   1955   -   1st   V clean copy with "The Beekeeper's Introit"

Fiction for children. OUP. Set in a Cathedral Choir School with bees, young people and the Bishop and his doings

20   -   20thC

492 McArthur, A E   *Swarm Trigger*

-      1984   -   1st   Paperback

The great secret revealed?? In brief it is claimed to be requeening each year after the main flow.

6   -   MOD

493 McFie, D   *Practical Beekeeping and Honey Production*

708   1936   1944?   nd   (5 copies)

A handbook for beginners. His "modern beehive" is the WBC.

5   5   20thC

494 McNichol, H   *The Young Beekeeper*

710   1953   1st   -   (3 copies-1with dw)

For boys. Mr Merry, a retired schoolmaster, introduces his 15 year old grandson Peter to beekeeping.

12   3   20thC

495 Mellor, I   *Honey*

-      1980   -   1st   hb (3 copies)

A collection of items of folk lore,poetry,fable and curious facts about bees and honey.

8   3   MOD

496 Metcalf, F H *The Bee Community*

718   1948   -   1st   (5 copies-1 with good dw)

:the study of an insect. Bee Craft..3 fine coloured plates and many other illustrations. Focuses on the individual bee,its structure and social life.

15   5   20thC

497

-

498 Metland, D *Honey Pure & Natural*

-      1985   -   1st   pb

Healthy eating guide. Recipes and remedies. Coloured photos.

5   -   MOD

499   Meyer, O   *The Beekeeper's Handbook*

-          1981   -   1st   Fair. Paperback

General Secretary of BBKA. He prepared the revised edition of Mace's Handbook of 1976. A useful manual for novices and experienced beekeepers. Just predates varroa in the UK. An elaboration of 'Basic Beekeeping'.(500)

10   -   MOD

---

500   Meyer, O   *Basic Beekeeping*

-          1978   -   1st&2nd imp.   (2 copies) pbs

Everything a beginner should know.

8   2   MOD

---

501   Meyer, O   *Microscopy on a Shoestring*

-          1984   -   1st   Mint hb dw

"intended as a reference book for the workbench of the keen amateur". User-friendly and conversational in style-"are you sitting comfortably?"

5   -   MOD

---

502   Miller, Wilbert   *Lets Build a Beehive*

-          1976   -   1st   Near mint

US hives plans and other DIY equipment. Very user-friendly.

10   -   USA

---

503   Milne, L & M   *The Senses of Animals & Men*

-          1963   -   1st   Torn dw

Indirect reference only. Praised by WH Auden. Explores senses other than the basic five.

12   -   20thC

---

504   Miner, T B   *The American Beekeeper's Manual*

266 J244   1849   1850   -   Slightly foxed o/w very clean

:being a Practical Treatise etc....the result of many years experience. Neatly illustrated. "The best all-round American bee-book till then published" (Walker). "By no means over-modest."(Dodd) He claimed that hitherto there had been no truly popular work because 'the subject was too dry' He offered his comprehensive work as "worthy of the confidence of the public" as"his success in the cultivation of this insect has been beyond precedent"

250   -   USA

---

505   Ministry of Agriculture & Fisheries
Report on Marketing of Honey and Beeswax in England and Wales

724   1931   -   1st   (2 copies -1 belonged to T Edwardes

25   2   20thC

---

506   Ministry of Agriculture & Fisheries(Butler)   *Beehives. Bulletin 144*

729   1949   1964   3rd   Fair

HMSO Describes National,Smith,Commercial and WBC hives

10   -   20thC

507a Ministry of Ag & Fish   *Beekeeping Bulletin No 9*
723   1930   1937   6th   (4 copies) Also 1944-11th Imp of 6th,revised.,1945-new ed by Colin Butler
A brief introduction to theory and practice
5   4   20ᵗʰC

507b Ministry of Ag & Fish   *Diseases of bees. Bulletin No 100*
727   1945   1945 1947 1st 1st reprint   (2 copies)
Diseases no longer part of bulletin no 9
5   2   20ᵗʰC

507c Ministry of Ag & Fish   *7 Collected leaflets*
1922   1924   2nd   -
WBC preferred. Encouragement to beginners.
5   -   20ᵗʰC

508   Mollan, R C *Reprinted Papers on Bee Husbandry*
-    1733   1980   Reprint   Royal Dublin Society
The Royal Dublin Society. 3 papers from Thorley(1767),Dobbs(1750) and Dublin Soc (1733). Thorley's 'Directions' are from The Gardener's New Companion. (See No 709)
20   -   ANT

509   More, Daphne   *Beekeeping*
-    1977   -   1st   pb Ex library
A good introduction in neat paperback format. Photographs by Frank Vernon.
8   -   MOD

510   More, Daphne   *The Bee Book*
731   1976   -   1st   (2 copies) pbs
:the history and natural history of the honeybee."A fascinating beekeeping compendium" (Showler) Knowledge of the craft detailed from Aristotle to the present day.
7   2   MOD

511   Morely, W S   *Beekeeping for Profit*
465   1914   1914   1st   -
8 excellent period photographs. Bar-framed hives.
25   -   OLD

512   Morely, W S   *Another*
465   1914   1914   1st
25   -   OLD

513   Morley, W M   *The Bee People*
436 j354 1907   1899   -   1st UK edition   -
Well illustrated. Written for children with the bee speaking directly to her readers about her life and work. This Methuen revised edition is considered inferior by Showler.
30   -   OLD

514 -   -
-       -   -

---

515 Morse, Prof R   *Honey Bee Pests, Predators, and Diseases*
-       1978   1980   2nd imp   dw slightly spotted o/w very clean copy
of Cornell Univ, New York. An international authority on bees. Editor of 'Gleanings' magazine. A remarkable compendium of contributions by 16 acknowledged experts. 'This is an outstanding new work…the standard text in its field'
25   -   USA

---

516 Naile, F   *The Life of Langstroth*
J368   1942   -   1st   dw. with magazines & letters on Langstroth
In 1953 George Hawthorne invited readers of The Dalesman to tell of any record of the Langstroth family, descended from Thomas of Horton, Ribblesdale. The response was two letters one which gives a family tree back to the late 17th century and the other packed with information about the family and its likely fate. These documents are included with Miss Naile's book together with a BBJ in which Dr Fraser comments briefly about Langstrothdale and Lorenzo. Miss Naile writes with great authority on his life and work.
70   -   USA

---

517 Neighbour, Alfred   *The Apiary*
307   1865   1866   2nd   -
:or Bees,bee-hives and bee culture. Alfred (b1825)was the famous son of George Neighbour who sold appliances near D Wildman in Holborn from 1814.He exhibited at the Great Exhibition in 1851, and also bought Tegetmeier's library of bee books. He imported Italian bees (1859). The book has numerous woodcuts and poems as well as a comprehensive account of bee culture.
90   -   OLD

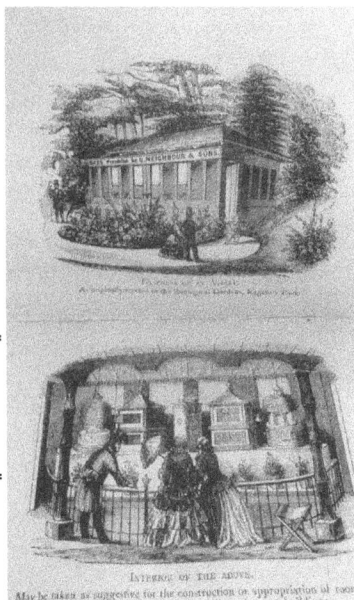

---

518 Neighbour, Alfred   *Another*
307   1865   1866   2nd   -   -
90   -   OLD

---

519 Neighbour, Alfred   *Another*
307   1865   1866   2nd   Some writing on   -
90   -   OLD

---

520 Nelson, J A   *The Embryology of the Honeybee*
470 J371   1915   -   1st   Princeton USA
Preface by Prof Phillips. Explores in scientific detail the development of the honey bee in its embryonic stages from egg to larva in 76 hours. 8 page list of references to sources. Brilliant illustrations of the development of the egg.
50   -   USA

---

521   Newman, Thomas G
Bees and Honey
J374   1882   c1900

Pub ABJ. Interesting engravings, picturing apiaries,plants, equipment etc. 11 pps of period advertisements, those for books showing him as the author of 10 publications

50   -   USA

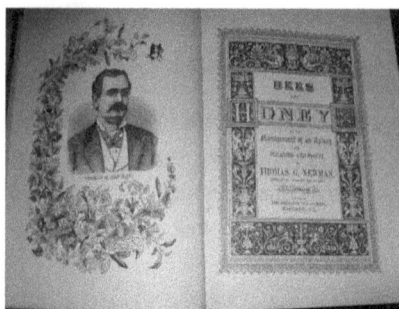

---

522   Nixon, G   The World of Bees
735   1954   -   1st   dw

Superbly illustrated by Arthur Smith. Coloured frontispiece and brilliant b&w drawings of British bees and wasps.

15   -   20

---

523   Nixon, G   Another
735   1954   -   1st   -   -

10   -   20

---

524   Nixon, G   Another
735   1954   -   -   pb No col frontispiece   -

4   -   20

---

525   Nobbs, S   Make Your Own Skep
-          1969   -   1st   Leaflet (2 copies)   :and revive a lost art.

5   2   20

---

526   Nutt, Thomas   Humanity to Honey Bees
215   1832   1837   4th   -

:the management of Honey-bees upon an improved and humane plan by which their lives may be preserved .(from death by sulphur fumes). Revised and edited by Rev Thos Clark.Nutt was a Wisbech lad "A drapers assistant of no great schooling" He was a stout advocate of collateral hives.first written about by Stephen White. Nutt also designed an 'Inverted Hive' and an observatory hive

100   -   ANT

---

527   Nutt, Thomas   Another
215   1832   1837   4th   -

100   -   ANT

---

528   Nutt, Thomas   Another
215   1832   1848   7th   -

Pub by J Leach for Nutt's widow. 32 pps of advertisements for books.

75   -   ANT

529   Oxenham, J   *Bees in Amber*

MT 27   1913   -   (6 copies)

A little book of thoughtful verse'. No direct bearing on bees or beekeeping.

5   6   OLD

530a Palmer, Ray *Bombus the Bumblebee*

739   1940   1956   -   Reprint

V good prints by Neave Parker. One of 8 'Animals All' books for children. Semi-anthropomorphic treatment. The bee has animal ways but its behaviour is described in human language.

20   2   20ᵗʰC

530b Palmer, Ray   *Another*

739   1940   1940   1st   dw   -

20   -   20ᵗʰC

531   Patterson, Robert   *Natural History of Bees in Shakespeare*

225   1838   1841   2nd   Slightly bumped but clean

Plate of Shakespeare. Upwards of 80 illustrations. A scholarly work

100   -   ANT

532   Pavord, A V   *Bees & Beekeeping*

741   1970   -   1st   pb (3 copies)

Cassells Pet and Fancy Books No 12

8   3   20ᵗʰC

533   Pavord, A V *Another*

741   1970   1975   -   hb (2 copies)   -

12   2   20ᵗʰC

534   Payne, J H *The Apiarian's Guide*

217   1833   1838   2nd   -

:containing practical directions for the management of bees upon the depriving system. Advocates the Cottage Hive, a flat-topped skep with boxes above - an early super. A respecter of Thos. Nutt and other writers such as Swammerdam,Bevan and Huish. 7 illustrations of skeps and collateral boxes. Concludes with a monthly guide.

100   -   ANT

535   Pellett, F   *Productive Beekeeping*

476 J403   1916   1918   2nd   (3 copies)

1879-1951 Associate editor of American Bee Journal. Iowa State Apiarist. Modern methods of production and marketing of honey. Lippincott's Farm Manuals. 134 illustrations mainly his own original photos.A valuable manual of its day which makes no claim to originality of method.

25   3   USA

536   Pellett, F   *Another*

476 J403   1916   1918   2nd   Rubbed   -

20   -   USA

537 Pellett, F   *Living from Bees*

J410   1944   1944   1st   Torn dw.

An interesting chapter on other US bee-masters and a good glossary of bee terminology.. All about beekeeping as a business.

25   -   USA

---

538 Pellett, F   *Another*

j410   1944   1946   Revised and enlargeddw small tear.

-

15   -   USA

A yield of 200 or more pounds of surplus honey is not unusual in a good location.

---

539 Pellett, F   *American Honey Plants*

j406   1920   1947   4th revised   dw.

together with those…of value..as a source of pollen. A greatly enlarged edition. Over 200 illustrations ,alphabetical and indexed under common and scientific names. A thorough work of authoritative scholarship.

25   -   USA

---

540 Pellett, F   *Practical Queen Rearing*

j404   1918   -   3rd   A clean copy

Pub ABJ. Simple methods briefly put for 'busy men'. Draws on Alley, Doolittle and Sladen.

30   -   USA

---

541 Perret-Maisonneuve, A   *L'apiculture Intensive et L'Elevage des Reines*   -

1923   1923   1st   French. A Sturges own copy. Limp covers and chipped spine

CP Dadant writes in the preface. The emphasis is on selection and queen rearing.

40   -   FOR

---

542 Pettigrew, A   *Handy Book of Bees*

318   1870   1870   1st

:being a practical treatise on their profitable management. The most famous skeppist who advocated an uncommonly large flat-topped basket. A Methodist and total abstainer in demand as a Band of Hope speaker. Sold hives for about 30 shillings each and would pay £1 and a new skep for a first swarm. This edition has 16pps of adverts for books.

85   -   OLD

543 Pettigrew, A *Another*

| 318 | 1870 | 1875 | 2nd | Revised and improved | - |
| 60 | - | OLD | | | |

544 Pettigrew, A *Another*

| 318 | 1870 | 1875 | 3rd | Revised and improved | - |
| 50 | - | OLD | | | |

545 Pettigrew, A *Another*

| 318 | 1870 | 1881 | 4th |
| 24 pps of adverts for books - with a new supplement (pps 145-178) |
| 50 | - | OLD |

546 Phillips, Dr E F *Beekeeping*

| 472 | j412 1915 | 1920 | - | Sturge's copy; rubbed |

:a discussion of the life of the honey bee. Leading American entomologist and teacher of beekeeping. 1878-1951 He donated his books to Cornell Univ Library and built on it as Professor of Apiculture. It was subsequently named in his honour.

| 30 | - | 20thC |

547 Phillips, Dr E F *Another*

| 472 | 1915 | 1920 | - | Knight's copy |
| 35 | - | 20thC |

548 Potter, A *The Killer Bees*

| - | 1977 | - | 1st | pb |

All about the African bees introduced to Brazil which created a major scare and a TV investigation in 1975.

| 10 | - | USA |

549 Powell, J *The World of a Beehive*

| - | 1979 | - | 1st | - |

An informative introduction to the organisation of the colony,the relationship with plants,the nature of honey and how to get started in beekeeping. Predates varroa.

| 15 | - | MOD |

550 Price, J *Price on Beekeeping*

| 745 | 1949 | - | 1st |

A weekly guide. 1872-1947 Published posthumously by Staffs BKA. Collected by G. St J Jones. "60 years of practical experience made him a complete bee-master".

| 15 | - | 20thC |

551 Prys-Jones,O and Corbet,SA *Bumblebees*

| - | 1987 | - | 1st | (2 copies) pbs |

Authoritative,scientific and intended to stimulate and encourage further research by giving basic taxonomic information and guidance on investigative techniques. Coloured plates

| 10 | 2 | MOD |

552 Quinby, Moses *Mysteries of Beekeeping*

j442   1853   1865   -   USA revised

:being a complete analysis of the whole subject etc. 1810-1875 He was born in the same year as Langstroth and became the first commercial beekeeper in the USA with 1200 stocks producing 10 tons of honey a year. His boxes had 8 frames with deep combs. He advocated nest boxes for wrens to keep wax moth at bay. Revisions of his book persisted till 1918 " Quinby's treatise appeared four year after Miner's and in the same year as that of Langstroth whose hive he afterwards adopted. It shows much careful observation and original thought. The author was highly esteemed; one of the best American writers" (Walker). He invented the Quinby smoker and the forerunner of Dadant frames. "One of the founding fathers of practical beekeeping in the United States" (Hooper).New directions in beekeeping pointed out,in a volume with neat helpful drawings

150   -   USA

553 Ransome, Hilda *The Sacred Bee*

747 j446 1937   1937   1937   1st   -

:in ancient times and folklore. 12 plates. A superb authoritative work. The title quotes a line from a poem by Charles Butler 1609.

70   -   20thC

554 Ransome, Hilda *Another*

747   1937   1937   1st   Sllightly sunned spine   -

70   -   20thC

555 Ratcliff, John *Beekeeper's Folly*

748   1949   1949   1st   Signed by author

An engineer. A manual for beekeepers with some experience. Emphasises good standard practice and the avoidance of mistakes and pitfalls.

15   -   20thC

556 Ratcliff, John *Another*

748   1949   1949   1st   (3 copies) -

10   3   20thC

557 Rayment, Tarleton *Money in Bees in Australasia*

477   1916   1925   2nd   -

Pub Whitcombe and Tombs,Melbourne. Well-illustrated.   Features the value of eucalypts and 'Wattles' -Acaciae. A greatly informative manual for the Australian beekeeper, amateur or commercial professional.

30   -   20thC

558 Redpath, N *A Guide to Keeping Bees in Australia*

-     1981   1985   3rd print -

An excellent basic manual for the 6000 registered beekeepers 'down under'.

20   -   MOD

559 Rendl, George *The Way of a Bee*

749   1933   1933   1st

For children. Translated by P Kirwan from Der Bienenroman. An Austrian beekeeper's son writes lyrically about a bee's life from a bee's point of view

| 12 | - | 20ᵗʰC | | |

---

560 Rendl, George   *Another*

| 749 | 1933 | 1933 | 1st | - |
| 12 | - | 20ᵗʰC | | |

---

561 Rendl, George   *Another*

| 749 | 1933 | 1935 | re-issued | |
Swan Lib
| 10 | - | 20ᵗʰC | | |

---

562 Rendl, George   *Another*

| 749 | 1933 | 1935 | re-issued | |
Swan Lib
| 12 | - | 20ᵗʰC | | |

---

563 Rendl, George   *Another*

| 749 | 1933 | 1935 | re-issued dw | |
Swan Lib
| 15 | - | 20ᵗʰC | | |

---

564 Reynolds, John   *Bees & Wasps*

| 751 | 1974 | 1980 | 4th imp | For children |
A beautifully presented book for young naturalists of 9 to 12 years
| 10 | - | 20ᵗʰC | | |

---

565 Ribbands, C R   *The Behaviour and Social Life of Honeybees*

| 752 | 1953 | 1953 | 1st | dw chipped |
Pub BRA. Always recommended for exam candidates and other students of beekeeping. 9 plates and 66 other illustrations. By the Principal Scientific Officer at Rothamsted. A review of published research supplemented by the author's own insights. Written in everyday English. 20 closely printed pages of scholarly references world-wide and a list of 450 authors quoted. Brilliant accessible science interlarded with poetry.
| 30 | - | 20ᵗʰC | | |

---

566 Ribbands, C R   *Another*

| 752 | 1953 | 1953 | 1st | - | - |
| 30 | - | 20ᵗʰC | | |

---

567 Ribbands, C R   *Another*

| 752 | 1953 | 1953 | 1st | dw. | - |
| 40 | - | 20ᵗʰC | | |

---

568 Ribbands, C R   *Another*

| 752 | 1953 | 1953 | 1st | dw slightly torn. Signed by author | - |
| 45 | - | 20ᵗʰC | | |

569 Richardson, H   *The Hive and the Honeybee*

259   1847   1852   new ed   Loose with plastic spine   Reading copy but complete. Quite scarce

: profits of beekeeping,diseases and enemies and remedies for them. The edition was enlarged by Westwood who adds hive data resulting from the Great Exhibition at the Crystal Palace in 1851

90   -   ANT

---

570 Richardson, H   *Another*

259   1847   1852   new ed   Bound with 239 and a book on gardening and a book on soils.

Price as per 239 (Ref No 384)

0   -   ANT

---

571 Riches, Dr H R C *Beekeeping*

756   1976   -   1st   (3 copies)

A Foyles Handbook giving concise basic information on beekeeping.

8   3   MOD

---

572 Robinson, James *British Bee Farming*

353   1880   -   1st   scarce

:its profits and pleasures. An anecdotal conversational style "so simple that any village beekeeper may with ease follow its teaching"

130   -   OLD

---

573 Robinson, James *Another*

353   1880   1889   2nd   -

130   -   OLD

---

574 Robinson, W P A *Making Your Garden Pay*

-          1953   1953   2nd imp   dw chipped

Bees pps 162-172"The art of beekeeping lies in persuading the Hive Mind that it wants what you want" (Making honey and not swarming).

12   -   20ᵗʰC

---

575 Rodionov & Shabarshov   *The Fascinating World of Bees*

-          1983   1986   1st UK   -

Translated from Russian by Maya Victorova. A fine 308 page account of bees and the craft in Russia with excellent colour photographs.. Langstroth hives.

10   -   MOD

---

576 Rohde, E S *Shakespeare's Wild Flowers*

760a   1935   -   1st   chipped dw

A handsome rare book. Watercolour reproductions from the V & A by Jacques le Moyne,circa 1570. A meticulous study of Shakespeare's usage

50   -   MISC

---

577 Rood, R N *Ants and Bees*

j460   1962   1975   5th   Large pb booklet

For older children as part of a binder collection for reference. Clear exposition and well illustrated.

8   -   USA

---

578   Root, A I   *Better Beekeeping*

j463   mid 1920s   -   Pamphlet

Amos Root (1839-1923) founded The AI Root Co. of Medina,Ohio in 1869. The company effectively created world-wide commercial beekeeping through standardisation and mass-production of appliances and comb foundation mills. A God-fearing man whose descendants enhanced the business and created the long-running authoritative masterpiece -ABC and XYZ. This is a promotional booklet to advertise the A I Root Company.

10   -   USA

---

579   Root, A I   *The ABC and XYZ of Bee Culture*

J494   1877   1895   -   -

"Arranged conveniently, encyclopedia fashion…every page is interesting….based upon the actual experience of a man who is at once a keen observer, a sympathetic friend to the bees and a most succesful apiarist" (Comstock) First published serially in Gleanings in Bee Culture which began in 1873 where AI Root ran an interactive column for 48 years

40   -   USA

---

580   Root, A I   *Another*

J494   1877   1903   -   Some small marginal notations

This and all the other editions are regularly updated to keep abreast of everything important in beekeeping - except the poetry as Sharp remarks.

40   -   USA

---

581   Root, A I   *Another*

J494   1877   1910   -   Fair

Root "not only made two blades of grass grow where one had grown before..he also made things grow where they had never grown before"(Medina County Gazette).[after Dean Swift]

20   -   USA

---

582   Root, A I   *Another*

J494   1877   1913   -   -   -

40   -   USA

---

583   Root, A I   *Another*

J494   1877   1917   -   Reading quality   -

10   -   USA

---

584   Root, A I   *Another*

J494   1877   1919   -   -   -

40   -   USA

---

585   Root, A I   *Another*

J494   1877   1947   -   -   -

25   -   USA

---

586   Root, A I   *Another*

J494	1877	1950	-	-	-
20	-	USA			

587   Root, A I   *Another*

J494	1877	1966	33rd	Reprint of 2nd edition

Still an enormously informative resource on all aspects of the craft. For example the evolution of American hives is lucidly explained

20	-	USA

588a   Root, A I   *Root Memorial Number*   *Vol X No 1*

1939	-	Frail but complete 41 page booklet

Celebrates the centenary of the birth of AI Root "In his later years AI Root was almost constantly in the attitude of prayer."

20	-	USA

588b   Root, A I   *The ABC and XYZ of Bee Culture*

J494	1877	1983	-	Mint reprint	-
20	-	USA			

590   Rowsell, H   *Henry's Bee Herbal*

762	1974	-	1st	Paperback

Optimistic applications of honey as therapy for many diseases.

6	-	20thC

591   Rusden, Moses   *A Further Discovery of Bees*

55	1679	1679	1st

Keeping (bees) in transparent boxes instead of straw hives…Published by His Majesties especial command and approved by the Royal Society…to be sold at his house next the sign of the King's Arms in Bowling Alley in Westminster. Beemaster to King Charles II. An apothecary and ally of Evelyn,the diarist. Rusden's boxes are similar to Gedde's octagon.Nice simple illustrations. Tickner Edwardes points out that he made the queen a king in deference to Charles and thought that pollen pellets were the actual materials of young bees.

600	-	ANT

592   Russian book on beekeeping -

-	1971	-	-	Near mint

In Russian. Beautiful illustrations. 432pps

10	-	FOR

593   Sammataro, Diana and Avilabile, Alphonse   *The Beekeeper's Handbook*

-	1978	1981	4th printing	Large pb

Univ. of Connecticut. Designed for absolute beginners with clear exposition, but also tackles some more advanced techniques.

15	-	USA

594   Samson, G Gordon   *Bees for Pleasure & Profit*

408   1892   1921   5th   (2 copies)One red cover, one green. Revised and enlarged

A guide to the manipulation of bees etc.Lockwood's Garden Manuals. Very thorough. BBJ grumbled that it was largely derivative,had errors,poor illustrations of bees and borrowed images from Blow's catalogue and Mr Cowan 'without acknowledgement'. This latter point is remedied in these revised editions.The provincial press not unjustly heaped praise on the book. Samson is most gracious about Cowan on p 76.

20   2   OLD

---

595   Samuelson, James   *The Honey Bee*

296   1860   1860   1st   v fine copy

;its natural history,habits,anatomy and microscopical beauties. Chapters on instinct and reason. 8 tinted lith. plates including bell-jar and microscope frontispiece.

65   -   OLD

---

596   Samuelson, James   *Another*

296   1860   - 1st   One loose page

-         60   OLD

---

597   Sandars, E   *The Insect Book for the Pocket*

-         1946   1951   2nd imp   Grey cover

pps 68-117 for bees. 25 pps of beautiful coloured plates of insects starting with bees.

10   -   MISC

---

598   Sandars, E   *Another*

-         1946   1951   2nd imp   . Pink cover   -

10   -   MISC

---

599   Sandeman Allen, A L   *Beekeeping with 20 Hives*

541   1952   -   1st   (3 copies -2 with chipped dws)

Bee Craft book. An accountant's view of cost-effective beekeeping. Favours Dadant hives. Recommends 10 books pps 116/7.

20   3   20thC

---

600   Saunders, Edward   *Wild Bees, Wasps and Ants*

438   1907   1907   1st   -

and other stinging insects. 4 col plates. Bees 1-87. Illustrated by Constance A Saunders. A remarkably plain and lucid style.

45   -   OLD

---

601   Saunders, Edward   *Another*

438   1907   1907   1st   Excellent -

35   -   OLD

---

602   Saunders, Edward   *Another*

438   1907   1907   1st   Excellent -

35   -   OLD

603   Sawyer, R   *Pollen Identification for Beekeepers*

| - | 1981 | - | 1st | (4 copies -2 with cards) Limp |

Excellent illustrations of pollen grains identifiable under a microscope with advice on how to do it.

| 10 | 4 | MOD |

---

604   Schlipf   *Landwork*

| - | 1847 | - | 1st | German. Loose pages. Paper covers |

Popular handbook

| 40 | - | FOR |

---

605   Schofield, Lt Col AN   *Teach Yourself Book*

| 764 | 1943 | - | Various hb & pb | (10 copies) |

A solicitor,praised by Colin Butler for abandoning old fallacies such as winter packing. Vernon's book replaced this in 1976.

| 5 | 10 | 20thC |

---

606   Scientific American (Von Frisch, Wilson, Wenner, Esch, Holldobler)   *Scientific American*

| - | 1962-1971 - | | reprints | 5 reprinted pamphlets. 4 on bee topics. | - |

| 15 | - | USA |

---

607   Scott,Amoret   *A Murmur of Bees*

| - | 1980 | - | 1st | (3 copies) |

Poetry about bees collected from classical and modern sources world-wide from over 3000 years of literature.

| 4 | 3 | MOD |

---

608   Scott, W   *Backyard Beekeeping*

| - | 1977 | - | 1st | (5 copies,3 green and 2 white covers) pbs |

A reader-friendly book for the novice. Bees,how to keep them, problems and recipes. Original drawings of character and do-it- yourself plans.

| 6 | 5 | MOD |

---

609   Scottish Beekeepers' Association   *An Introduction to Bees and Beekeeping*

| 767 | 1973 | - | 1st | pb Sold together with 4 four- page papers (1929) by experts. |

A brief but concise, richly informative manual made particularly relevant to Scotland. Useful bibliography and a guide to using the famous Moir Library,George IV Bridge,Edinburgh 1

| 10 | - | MOD |

---

610   Scottish Beekeepers' Association   *Another*

| 767 | 1973 | 1980 | revised | (2 copies) pbs | - |

| 5 | 2 | MOD |

---

611   Sechrist, Edward L   *Amateur Beekeeping*

| 768 j524 1955 1955 | 1976 | 2nd | (2 copies -1 ex lib) |

"Made suitable for use in Great Britain" by AC Brown. Sensible, readily understandable advice for beginners.

15   2   20ᵗʰC

---

612 Sechrist, Edward L   *Another*

768   1955   1958   1st UK   No dw Ex lib   -

8   -   20ᵗʰC

---

613 Seidel, Dr D   *Wild Flowers*

-    1978   -   -   Mint. Paperback   -

5   -   MISC

---

614 Sharp, D   *Insects - Part 2*

419   1899   1901   -   -

The Cambridge Natural History. Apidae pps10-70. Illustrated. Scientific anatomical descriptions of Anthrophita (bees)

25   -   OLD

---

615 Sharp, Dallas   *The Spirit of the Hive*

j528   1925   -   1st   Rubbed

:contemplations of a beekeeper. "The ABC and XYZ (of Root) is a good book. It tells you everything about the bees-except the poetry" "The whole work of keeping bees is instinct with wonder and beauty and romance" he says. A rhapsodical offering.. The rational humorists, Sellars and Yeatman, however, suggested that the scientific truth about bees is 'unpleasant' The hive is a highly mechanised unit and the bee is an entirely unsuitable subject for romantic affection or any sort of poetical affectation".

20   -   USA

---

616 Sharp, Dallas   *Another*

j528   1925   -   1st   -   -

25   -   USA

---

617 Sheehan, A *The Bumblebee*

-    1976   1977   Reprint   For children

For children. Very sharp and attractive coloured illustrations by Maurice Pledger.

10   -   MOD

---

618 Shipley, A   *Studies in Insect Life*

-    1916   1916   1st   Bees in chapters 2/3/4   -

25   -   MISC

---

619 Showler, K   *The Observation Hive*

-    1978   -   1st   (2 copies with dws)

:its history, construction, use and maintenance. By the IBRA Technical Expert-the leading Authority on bee-books and bookmen.

6   2   MOD

---

620 Shuckard, William   *British Bees*

309   1866   1866   1st   Loose spine

:an introduction to the study of the natural history of the bees indiginous to the British Isles. 16 superb coloured plates. 'They make the identification of the bees portrayed quite easy' (Fraser) Apis mellifera pps 321-362

50   -   OLD

---

621   Shuckard, William   *Another*

309   1866   1866   1st   -
50   -   OLD

---

622   Shuckard, William   *Another*

309   1866   -   1st   -   -
80   -   OLD

---

623   Simmins, Samuel   *A Modern Bee Farm*

395   1887   1914   4th   (3 copies-one with detached spine)

and its economical management etc. From Rottingdean,Sussex. The 1914 edition tackles bee paralysis or the Isle of Wight disease. Well-illustrated including a Jersey cow. Many testimonials from UK and USA, adverts for queens, journals,chickens and a cure for IoW disease. Two prices 6/- and 7/6.

25   3   OLD

---

624   Simmins, Samuel   *Another*

395   1887   1928   5th

No cow or adverts. Still prefers frames larger than standard for commercial purposes.(16X10"). The final version. 'Many beekeepers looked to Simmins as their oracle'(Fraser) His hives were operated from the rear like a chest of drawers but tended to stick with propolis.

35   -   OLD

---

625   Simmins, Samuel   *Another*

395   1887   1928   -

Now 10/- Still favours Izal to combat foul brood.

35   -   OLD

---

626   Sinclair, Dr D   *Life of the Honeybee*

-     1969   -   1st   (4 copies)

Ladybird Book "Concise clear text and high-quality illustrations…the most widely read of any English language bee book. (Showler) For children.

5   4   MOD

---

627   Skilling, Robert NH   *Sixty Years with Smoker & Veil*

-     1991   -   1st   Booklet

Reminiscences and tips by the Editor of 'The Scottish Beekeeper'. "Never disturb the brood nest" Pub NBB

5   -   MOD

---

628   Sladen, FWL   *Queen Rearing in England*

433   1905   1982   of 2nd ed   Facsimile edition. NBB.

with notes on…worker bees and how pollen is collected etc. He was a noted queen rearer of British Goldens. 'He was made Canadian Dominion Apiarist and drowned while in the execution of his duties' (Walker)

10   -   OLD

---

629   Sladen, FWL   *Another*

433   1905   1913   2nd   hardback ex lib

Coloured frontispiece of Golden Bees

15   -   OLD

---

630   Sladen, FWL   *Another*

433   1905   -   2nd   (2 copies) limp

Coloured frontispiece of Golden Bees

10   2   OLD

---

631   Sladen, FWL   *Another*

433   1905   -   1st   No cover -

15   -   OLD

---

632   Smailes, R   *Raise Your Own Queens.*

-        1970   1977   -   2nd edition

:by the 'punched cell' method. A well-illustrated leaflet

3   -   MOD

---

633   Smart, John   *Instructions for Collectors*

-        1940   1954   3rd revised   Insects British Museum

How to catch,kill,preserve and pack insects

20   -   MISC

---

634   Smith, F   *Catalogue of British Hymenoptera in the British Museum*

283   1855   1876   2nd   Ex-library. Slight foxing

11 plates delicately drawn. 2nd ed takes account of 'many important additions to our knowledge'

50   -   OLD

---

635   Smith, F G   *Beekeeping*

776   1963   -   1st   Soiled

:a beginner's guide to profitable honey and beeswax production. OUP Tropical Handbooks. Photographs and text promote beekeeping world-wide rather than UK.

10   -   20thC

---

636   Smith, Jay   *Better Queens*

j540   1949   1949   1st   (2 copies)

b1871 Tells how he does things, not how they should be done. An authority on queen-rearing.

35   2   USA

---

637   Smith, Jay   *Queen Rearing Simplified*

j540   1923   1923   1st   Spine rubbed. Gift to Sturges signed

From Indiana ."nothing new or radically different is offered". Just good advice for amateurs and professionals alike. Pub Root.

35	-	USA

---

638 **Smith, Victor J** *Down Among the Bee Folk*

777	1946	1946	1st	(2 copies)

One of the first post-war books for children Moralistic with an explicit Christian message throughout.

| 10 | 2 | 20thC |

---

639 **Smith, Victor J** *Another*

777	1946	-	1st	dw	-

| 15 | - | 20thC |

---

640 **Smith, Victor J** *Another*

777	1946	-	-	-	-

| 10 | - | 20thC |

---

641 **Snelgrove, LE** *Swarming, its Control and Prevention*

779	1934	((6 copies-various editions and conditions)

All privately printed.3rd and 7th editions have amendments to the original text

| 8 | 6 | 20thC |

---

642 **Snelgrove, LE** *Another*

779	1934	1946	9th	Signed by Illingworth

The book ran to 13 editions.

| 10 | - | 20thC |

---

643 **Snelgrove, LE** *Another*

779	1934	1945	8th	Spine badly repaired

1878-1965 A Headmaster and Inspector of Schools for Somerset. BBKA lecturer and judge. President 1956. Invented the complex Snelgrove System of artificial swarming. He was one of Nature's gentlemen" (Brown).

| 6 | - | 20thC |

---

644 **Snelgrove, LE** *Another*

779	1934	1981	13th	paperback

10th and subsequent editions revised by author.

| 10 | - | 20thC |

---

645 **Snelgrove, LE** *The Intro. of Queen Bees*

780	1940	1943	2nd	(2 copies)+H696

He devised the 'water method' of queen introduction. "A wet queen is readily accepted" he says. "A variety of methods suited to all circumstances" (Illingworth). The reader is spoilt for choice.

| 15 | 2 | 20thC |

---

646 **Snelgrove, LE** *Another*

780	1940	1943	2nd	Damage to spine. HB-

| 8 | - | 20thC |

---

647 Snelgrove, LE *Another*

780   1940   1943   2nd   Sunned cover.Otherwise good   -

10   -   20ᵗʰC

---

648 Snelgrove, LE *Another*

780   1940   1948   3rd   -

20   -   20ᵗʰC

---

649 Snelgrove, LE *Queen Rearing*

781   1946   1946   1st   hb A very clean copy

Pub by his daughter.A comprehensive immediate post-war update.

20   -   20ᵗʰC

---

650 Snelgrove, LE *Another*

781   1946   1981   4th   pb

Cites 98 sources from the beekeeping literature

20   -   20ᵗʰC

---

651 Snodgrass, R E *The Skeleto-Muscular Mechanisms of the Honey Bee*

782b   1942   1942   1st   pb

1875-1962 One of Prof EF Phillips' eminent researchers.His 'papers (over 80) are still widely cited and his drawings and diagrams were done with great care and precision' (Hooper)

20   -   USA

---

652 Snodgrass, R E *Anatomy of the Honeybee*

782a   1910   1956   new ed

"Not a revision (of Ref no 655) but an almost entirely rewritten account of the honey bee .in all its stages.

30   -   USA

---

653 Snodgrass, R E *Another*

782a   1910   1910   1st   Nicely re-bound. Flyleaf missing

Pub US Dept of Agriculture

50   -   USA

---

654 Snodgrass, R E *Another*

782a   1910   1910   1st   pb Signed Tickner Edwardes

The book ran to 13 editions.

40   -   USA

---

655 Snodgrass, R E *Anatomy and Physiology of the Honeybee*

782a   1910   1925   1st ed. 4th impression   -

Pub McGraw-Hill

30   -   USA

---

656 Snodgrass, R E *Another*

782a   1910   1925   1st ed. 6th impression   -

Pub McGraw-Hill
25   -   USA

---

657   Spiller, J   *The House Apiary*
784   1952   -   1st   (2 copies with dws)
:the many advantages of. Well-argued and generously illustrated with photos,plans and sketches.
15   2   20ᵗʰC

---

658   Stadlaender, C   *Honey Cookery*
-       1967   1978   4th   pb
over 100 pages of recipes
5   -   20ᵗʰC

---

659   Steiner, R   *Nine Lectures on Bees*
787   1929   1933   Limited edition number 544   -
given in 1923 to the workmen at the Goethanum. Anthroposophical Agric. Foundation. Meant to give some
understanding of the spiritual relationships in nature".
25   -   20ᵗʰC

---

660   Step, E   *Marvels of Insect Life*
-       No date   -   -   -
Fine colour plates
20   -   20ᵗʰC

---

661   Step, E   *Bees, Wasps and Ants and Allied Insects in the British Isles*
788   1932   1932   1st   dw browned
44 col plates and 170 photos. A beautiful book in the Wayside and Woodland Series. Mr Step died shortly after
completing the MS
30   -   20ᵗʰC

662a Step, E   *British Insect Life*
-       ND 1930's -   -   (2 copies) Handsome books
Bees on pages 184-221
15   2   20ᵗʰC

662b Stratton-Porter, Gene   *The keeper of the bees*
522 J433 1925   1926   2nd   -
The 135,000th sold. Novel with a US setting for a war veteran.
10   -   20ᵗʰC

---

663   Stephens-Potter, L   *The Beekeeper's Manual*
-       1984   -   1st   (2 copies with dws)
The author's pride! An accessible beginner's manual,easy to follow dealing with basics rather than more specialised
or complex techniques. Predates the arrival of varroa
10   2   MOD   -

---

664   **Stevens, Charles & Liebault, Jean**   *Maison rustique or The Countrie Farme*

16   1600   1600   1st   -

Stevens = Estienne. Translated by Richard Surflet, physician. One of three great sixteenth century encyclopaedias of rural economy. Estienne's 'Praedium Rusticum' (Paris 1554) was translated into French by Liebault in 1570. "English beekeepers were determined to stick to their good old Saxon ways...the English translation had no great success" (Fraser)

600   -   ANT

---

665   **Stevens, Frank**   *Adventures in Hiveland*   426   1903   1903   1st

For children. Illustrated by LA Sargent. Stars 'Nameless' the elf, bees and Victorian children. Much incidental instruction in bee-lore ensues.

30   -   OLD

---

666   **Stevens, Ken**   *Apiculture for Schools*

-          1977   1977   1st   Signed by author

Duplicated typescript with photographs and drawings. An excellent textbook for upper junior and secondary project work, for school bee clubs and their teachers. By the Kent County Bee Instructor.

10   -   MOD

---

667   **Stevens, Ken**   *Another*

-          1977   1977   1st   -

10   -   MOD

---

668   **Stevens, Ken**   *Alphabetical Guide Vol 2*

-          1985   1985   1st   Rare. Dw

A major magnificent and much undervalued work of scholarship and patient, thorough compilation from many sources. Comprehensive and redolent of good sense and wide knowledge.

50   -   MOD

---

669   **Stevens, Ken**   *Alphabetical Guide Vol 1*

-          1977   1977   1st   -

A dictionary of bee words. Duplicated script. Many helpful drawing. Useful as a companion to 666.

15   -   MOD

---

670   **Stevens, Ken**   *Another*

-          1977   1977   1st   Plastic spine binding

Privately printed. 235 pps

15   -   MOD

---

671   **Stevens, Ken**   *Another*

-          1977   1977   1st

Vol 1 is a small study compared to Vol 2

15   -   MOD

---

672   **Stevens, Ken**   *Alphabetical Guide Vol 1*

-          1977   1977   1st   Fair   -

10   -   MOD

---

673 **Storch, H**   *At the Hive Entrance*

-    1985   -   1st English   (2 copies)

Trans F Celis. An account of what the perceptive beekeeper can learn about the bees without opening the hive

8   2   MOD

---

674 **Struf**   *Agriculture*

-    -   -   -   German. 2 volumes. Bees in volume 2

1799-1825 Engraving of a bee-house on title page

150   -   FOR

---

675 **Stuart, F**   *City of the Bees*

792   1947   1947   1st   (4 copies)

"In the translucent light of waxen streets, a golden throng etc etc". Nature's high drama told in high-flown rhapsodic style!

12   4   20thC

---

676 **Stuart, F**   *Another*

792   1947   1951   -   -   -

10   -   20thC

---

677 **Stuart, F**   *Another*

792   1947   1953   -   -   -

10   -   20thC

---

678 **Stuart, F**   *Beekeeping Practice*

791   1945   1946   2nd   (2 copies) dw

The Managing Director of a honey company offers sound standard advice for post-war beekeepers. Advocated WBCs.

6   2   20thC

---

679 **Stuart, F**   *Another*

791   1945   -   3rd   dw. (4 copies)   -

6   4   20thC

---

680 **Stuart, F**   *Another*

791   1945   -   1st   dw (3 copies)   -

6   3   20thC

---

681 **Sturges, A M**   *Practical Beekeeping*

513   1924   -   1st   dw.

A handsome volume with a fine coloured frontispiece. A Sussex man, born 1879, wrote about his 'Shenstone' hive. It was very large, capable of copious insulation in vogue when hives were wrapped up for the winter with 'quilts'. It lacked ordinary WBC inner boxes. Wadey wrote a celebration of his life in 'Behaviour of Bees and Beekeepers'.

15   -   20thC

---

682   Sturges, A M   *Another*

513	1924	-	1st	-
18	-	20thC		

683   Sturges, A M   *Another*

513	1924	-	1st	Spine torn. O/w good. Authors dedication to Tickner Edwardes.

Edwardes helped him with his first chapter.

20	-	20thC		

684   Sturges, A M   *Another*

513	1924	-	1st	-	-
18	-	20thC			

685   Sturges, A M
The Rational System of Bee-keeping: for the prevention of disease and avoidance of swarming

507	1923	-	2nd	Pamphlet. 60 pps.

Sturges' first work. East Dean Apiaries.

10	-	20thC	

686   Sturges, A M   *Swarm Control and Comb Honey Production*

793	1927	-	1st	61 pps.

Has advertisements for his 50 shilling Shenstone Hive. His golden rule: 'Keep your colonies strong'.

15	-	20thC	

687   Sutherland, G   *Bees*

-	1977	-	1st	Book of 14 art prints

A fine book of 14 art prints. Remarkable work by a famous artist. "Art is hidden in Nature, he who can pull it out has found it"

15	-	MOD	

688   Swammerdam, J
The Book of Nature

111	1737	1758	1st ed in English	Folio volume

. Cover slightly loose

Translated T Flloyd. When Swammerdam turned his attention to the study of bees it gave a yield unequalled in any of his earlier work. He died in 1680 but the vital 2nd edition was not published until 1737. "The most important scientific work of the second half of the eighteenth century. It is a marvellous book " (Fraser) 'The anatomical illustrations...are still considered almost faultless. (IBRA)

800	-	ANT

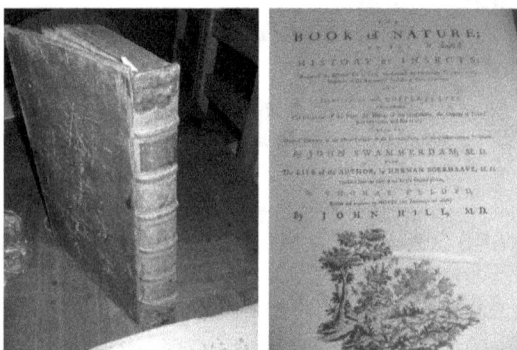

---

689   Taylor   *Bees for Beginners*

508	1923	no date	-	Blue cover. Later ed. (3 copies).

Appliance makers. Author Sir William Gavin. Frontispiece is a reproduction from W White 1771.

4	3	20thC

---

690   Taylor   *Another*

508	1923	1923	1st	Grey cloth

Basic help, avoiding controversy, in simple language. Favours WBC, supers and sections.

20	-	20thC

---

691   Taylor   *Another*

508	1923		2nd	Yellow cloth. Edwardes' presentation copy.-

20	-	20thC

---

692   Taylor   *Another*

508	1923	-	-	Red cloth -

15	-	20thC

---

693   Taylor, Henry   *The Beekeepers Manual*

227	1838	1860	6th	-

:or practical hints on the management etc. Describes the castes of bees, skeps and hives. First treatment of bee pasturage and seasonal management. "It is a volume that no apiculturist should be without" (Sunday Times)

110	-	ANT

---

694 **Taylor, Henry** *Another*

227	1838	1860	6th	-	-

110	-	ANT

---

695 **Taylor, Henry** *Another*

227	1838	1839	2nd	A very clean copy	-

150	-	ANT

---

696 **Taylor, Henry** *Another*

227	1838	1850	4th	-

Printed cover. Many advertisements

120	-	ANT

---

697 **Taylor, Henry** *Another*

227	1838	1855	5th	-	-

100	-	ANT

---

698 **Taylor, Henry** *Another*

227	1838	1880	7th	one loose gathering o/w good

An appendix containing long extracts from Evans' poem 'The Bees' (IBRA No 170) included by Alfred Watts who modernised the work.

90	-	ANT

---

699 **Taylor, Richard** *Beeswax Molding and Candle Making*

-	No date	-	-	pb

Helpful photographs

8	-	USA

---

700 **Taylor, Richard** *The Comb Honey Book*

-	1981	-	1st	pb

About getting good sections by using the 'shook swarm' method.

7	-	USA

---

701 **Taylor, Richard** *The Joys of Beekeeping*

796	1974	1976	1st UK	(2 copies with dws)

Philosophical musings on the beauty of the pursuit and the ordering of the hive Artistic illustrative drawings.

15	2	USA

---

702 **Taylor, Richard** *The How-to-do-it Book of Bee-keeping.*

-	1974	-	1st	pb

Helpful photos and readable style

10	-	USA

703 **Taylor, E H Ltd** *Catalogues*

- - - - (5 items).

Magnificent pamphlets. All the appliances illustrated. 'A book of reference....a beekeepers' Baedeker'. Two WW2 catalogues, also one 1947 (damaged) and three furniture and poultry catalogues.

6 - 20thC

704a Taylor, E H Ltd   *Catalogue of Beekeepers Supplies*

-          1920-1930 -   -   Varying conditions from mint (1922) to well used with damaged covers (1920) of which there are 6.

Catalogues of bees, hives and appliances. No issues for '24, '27 or '29 o/w complete set of 20 copies. All superbly illustrated and in direct evolution from Blow's issues from 1880 (see lot number 40). Internal evidence suggests that this collection was used for reference when updating catalogues in Taylor's offices. Includes an invoice 1919.

90 - 20thC

704b Taylor, E H Ltd   *Good Beekeeping*

- - - - (2 copies)

A monthly appliance dealer's magazine with seasonal advice and instructive articles by experts.

5 2 MISC

---

705 Taylor, E H Ltd   *Beekeeping equipment*

- - - - (5 issues)

1975 onwards. 1988 is centennial issue with the story of Blow and Taylor.

10 - 20thC

---

706 Teale, Edwin Way   *Grass Root Jungles*

-          1937   1944   -   Revised edition

A Book of Insects. 130 photos by the author. Quotes Izaak Wallton "If you like not the writing I commend you to the pictures" - with perfect justice.   Printed in US, pub Hale in London

15 - 20thC

---

707 Teale, Edwin Way   *The Golden Throng*

797 J557   1942   1940   1946   -   (8 copies)

:a book about bees. The large format edition has 85 excellent photographs by the author. Slightly literary style and many references to other writers. Bibliography.

6 8 20thC

---

708 The Nature Conservancy Council   *The Conservation of Bees & Wasps*

-          1979   -   -   Pamphlet

Concerns the importance of positive recognition of bees and wasps by the conservation movement.

3 - MOD

---

709 Thorley, Rev John   *The Gardeners New Companion*

97   1767   -   1st   Spine broken in half.

An unusual book not noted in IBRA Bibliography. By order of the Dublin Society, J Exshaw in Dame St. Has an excellent cut 'A Chinese Palace of Bees'

250 - ANT

---

710 Thorley, Rev John   *The Female Monarchy*

97   1744   -   1st   -

Melisselogia. Thorley was a Presbyterian clergyman of Chipping Norton. His book has pious moral lessons and is warmly appreciative of George II. It has a list of subscribers and makes unauthorised use of Cesi's illustration of the three castes, the first made with the help of a microscope. It has illustrations of octagonal hives and describes how he removed two queens from a swarm clustered on his maid's neck. He famously recommended using puff-ball narcotic to stupefy bees.

400   -   ANT

---

711   Thorley, Rev John   *Another*

97   1744   -   1st   -   -
400   -   ANT

---

712   Thorley, Rev John   *Another*

97   1744   -   -   Poor. Picture of Thorley a photocopy. Spine has 2" hole   -
200   -   ANT

---

713   Thorley, Rev John   *Another*

97   1744   1772   3rd   Front over detached
Issued by Thorley's son. Shows a fanciful Chinese Palace of Bees.
350   -   ANT

---

714   Thorley, Rev John   *Another*

97   1744   1774   4th   Bound with 789 and 756 Price as per 756 -
0   -   ANT

---

715   Tinsley, J   *Beekeeping Up-to-date*

801   1945   -   3rd   Mauve.
Distinguished Staffordshire beekeeper who did research into queen mating and wintering' (Dodd). Lecturer at W of Scot Agric Coll.
8   -   20thC

---

716   Tinsley, Joseph   *Another*

801   1945   -   3rd   Red cloth.
8   -   20thC

---

717   Tinsley, Joseph   *Another*

801   1945   -   2nd   Green cloth.
8   -   20thC

---

718   Tinsley, Joseph   *Another*

801   1945   -   2nd   Brown cloth.
8   -   20thC

---

719   Todd, H E   *Bobby Brewster's Bee*

801	1972	1983	3rd imp	Mint

For children. A modern fairy tale. Bobby is an ordinary schoolboy to whom extraordinary things happen (preface)

8	-	20th C

720   Tomlinson, C&S
Lessons from the Animal World

255	1846	1847	2nd	Covers weak. Ink stain

The bee as an example of economy. Pub by Society for Promoting Christian Knowledge. Hive, bumble and solitary bees. Frontispiece of swarm and skeps by Whimper.

40	-	ANT

721   Tompkins, Enoch & Griffith, Roger   *Practical Beekeeping*

-	1977	1981	8th	8th printing. Pb

Contributions to a helpful manual by over a dozen experts. Concentrated information for beginners and others. Pub Garden Ways.

12	-	USA

722   Tompkins, Enoch & Griffith, Roger   *Another*

-	1977	-	1st	pb	-

12	-	USA

723   Tonsley, C   *Honey for Health*

802	1969	1973	Rev. and enlarged ed Fair. Paperback

Editor of BBJ, chairman BBKA, bee farmer and judge. Recipes and medicinal uses.

2	-	20th C

724   Tusser, Thomas   *Five Hundred Pointes of Good Husbandrie*

3	1557	1812	-

An East Anglian farmer. Mentions bees only three times in his verses-swarming, drivi 19/20,64 and 155.

300	-	ANT

725   Unknown Author   *Who Was the First Architect ?*

328	1874	1888	-	-

or, Bees and bee-hives. 40 illustrations. Excellent coloured frontispiece with mother, children and skeps. Pub Nelson

40	-	OLD

726   Unknown Author   *Insects and their*

Habitations

220   1833   1846   15th   -

Children's book by SPCK A penny monthly magazine devoted to the improvement…of the industrious classes. A wonderful righteous compendium of household, physical and moral self-improvement. 'Heaven helps those who help themselves' Moral lessons: Like the busy bee/In books or works or healthy play/Let my first years be past/That they may give me every day/Some good account at last. Bees treated on a monthly basis. Contents list said to be readily converted into exam questions- on modern educational lines !! Bees ps 6-34 illustrated

100   -   ANT

727a Unknown Author   *The Family Economist*

-    1849   -   ? Ist   Nicely bound but top of spine chipped. Foxed end papers

Self-improvement manual. Includes a page of mottoes. "Men in savage life are ignorant of books" and "Love labour; if you need it not for food you do for physic" for example. Instructions for beekeepers given on a monthly basis. A delight to read on gardening and the 'Good Life'. The young wife's secret turns out to be that the 'surest way to avoid a second quarrel is never to have had a first'.

40   -   ANT

727b Unknown Author   *Remarkable insects*

242   1842   1842   1st   Small pocket book

Pub by the Religious Tract Society (founded 1799) Accurate information for the young with moral motives.

40   -   ANT

---

728 Urquhart, F A   *Introducing the Insect*

-    1949   1965   Rev. UK ed.   dw.

An introduction to entomology. Associate professor at Univ. of Toronto.

15   -   20thC

---

729 Urquhart, J   *Keeping Honeybees*

-    1978   -   1st   Limp

Penny-Pinchers Booklet. A straightforward, uncomplicated primer for beginners

5   -   MOD

---

730 Valli & Summers   *Honey Hunters of Nepal*

-    1988   -   -

A remarkable large book. Magnificent photographs of magnificent people in equally magnificent settings.

15   -   MOD

---

731 Various Authors   *The Complete Farmer*

117   1766   1769   2nd   -

A general dictionary of husbandry together with the manner of raising bees. Draws on Gedde,Warder,Thorley,Reaumur etc. Plate III shows hives. Date 1769 differs for 2nd Ed from IBRA (1767)

350   -   ANT

---

732 Vernon, F   *Hogs at the Honeypot*

-    1981   -   1st   Paperback. Signed by author

About Hampshire beekeeping by the 'Teach Yourself' author. Pub BBNO Historic references e.g

Butler,Worlidge,Gilbert White,poems and loving recollections of Hampshire bee-masters

8   -   MOD

---

733 Vernon, F   *Teach Yourself Beekeeping*

806   1976   -   1st, 3rd   Paperback. 1 signed. (7 copies).

Successor to Schofield, the second author in the series. 'First-class lecturer, beekeeper, photographer and linguist.' (Stevens). An Anglo-French County Apiarist and Disease Officer for the Min of Ag.

5   7   20thC

---

734 Vesey-FitzGerald, B   *The World of Ants, Bees & Wasps*

807   1969   -   1st   -

An introduction to the inconceivable for those who have not lost the sense of wonder'. The amazing discovered in the commonplace.

15   -   20thC

---

735 Veterinary Historical Society   *Vetinary Bulletin 1982/3*

-    1982   -   -   Lecture by N. Comben

Report of a valuable shrewd lecture on collecting books by a celebrated expert on old farming and farriery books.

5   -   BAB

---

736 Virgil *Bees 4th Georgic*

268   1861   1880   -   -

Publius Virgilius Maro. Bohn's Classical Library. Trans. By Davidson, revised byTA Buckley. Contains The Georgics and The Aeneid. Spoke of two queens, good and bad, in the same hive. Says bees gather their young from plants, carry stones as ballast in high winds, commends clipping the King, recognises robbing by rival 'armies 'and says hives are made of cork or osiers. Some sound advice given. "Gargle your mouth with a draught of water and bear in your hand before you the searching smoke" .'Virgil looked on bees with the eyes of the small-holder and speaks of what he understands '(Fraser) Edwardes says 'The Georgics is the first book that should be given to a beginner in apiculture'. Sellars and Yeatman however poke fun at his 'hysterical information' "They sharpen their stings, he tells us, on their beaks, and do not breed like other animals but 'find' their eggs", and he states that since bees cannot swim "it is essential to place stepping stones in all the neighbouring streams". Maybe Virgil was just making sure they had water.

50   ·-   OLD

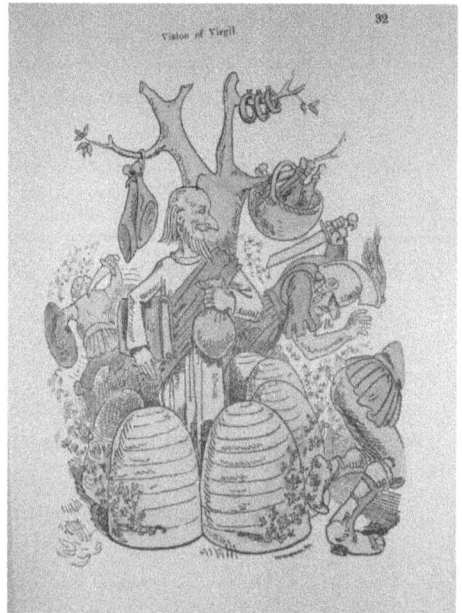

Vision of Virgil   32

---

737 Von Frisch   *Bees: Their vision, chemical senses and language*

637 J183   1927   1951   3rd   Spine rubbed

1886 -1982 Professor of Munich University (1925) and sometime President of the IBRA

12   -   USA

738   Von Frisch   *Another*

637 J183   1927   1950   1st USA ed   dw chipped. Clean copy

Foreword by Dr D Griffin of Cornell.. The text is made from three lectures given by Von Frisch in the USA in 1949. Well illustrated.

15   -   USA

---

739   Von Frisch   *Another*

637   J183   1950 US   1968   -   Ex-library

Co-winner of a Nobel prize for his work on the directional dances of bees and their senses and communications. 'A straightforward account that requires…neither technical background not undue effort'. The text of 3 lectures in the USA.

15   -   20thC

---

740   Von Frisch   *Animal Architecture*

-            1975   -   1st   dw.

Surveys the creative building activity of animals of all species. 'Intended for a non-specialised audience… to help protect our living environment against the destruction that threatens it' (Dr. Griffin, Cornell Univ.).

20   -   20thC

---

741   Von Frisch   *The Dancing Bees*

638   1954   1955   2nd USA ed.   (2 copies)

Readers union edition. Translated Dora Ilse. A masterly and readable account of the secrets of the bee civilisation.

15   2   20thC

---

742   Von Frisch   *Another*

638   1954   1954   -   -

First English

15   -   20thC

---

743   Von Frisch   *Another*

638   1954   1966   -   -

Ilse & Walker. Revisions and additions made in the 7th German edition.

15   -   20thC

---

744   Vosnjak, M   *The Miracle of Propolis*

-            1978   1980   3rd Imp   pb

A story about the healing properties of propolis on a Jugoslavian church painter, Rado Siefert.

8   -   MOD

---

745   Wadey, H J   *The Bee Craftsman*

810   1943   1943   1st   (4 copies)

:a short guide to the life story and management of the honeybee. A Bee Craft book. 6 editions in all. Wadey was editor of Bee Craft for many years to 1972.He managed up to 120 stocks over 20 years. Lecturer and humorist.

3   4   20thC

746   Wadey, H J   *Another*

| 810 | 1943 | - | 2nd | (3 copies - 2 with dws) | - |
| 3 | 3 | 20thC | | | |

747   Wadey, H J   *Another*

810   1943   -   3rd   (2 copies) -

3   2   20ᵗʰC

748   Wadey, H J   *Another*

810   1943   1978   6th rev.   Paperback. (2 copies).   -

3   2   20ᵗʰC

749   Wadey, H J   *The Behaviour of Bees and of Beekeepers*

812   1948   -   1st   (4 copies - all with dws)

Wadey has fun with the craft and its practitioners.

7   4   20ᵗʰC

750   Wadey, H J   *Introducing Beekeeping*

811   1946   -   1st   (2 copies - 1 with dw)

A book for the novice. Pub. Bognor Regis.

10   2   20ᵗʰC

751   Walker, Lt. Col H J O
Catalogue of Bee Books collected and
offered for sale by Lt. Col H.J.O. Walker

814   1929   1985   -   Handsomely bound including a collector of honey jar labels. Ashforth's copy

Pub NBB. A remarkable catalogue which has endured as a bibliography and reference book of international importance. Walker (1843-1934) sold his Library as a single lot. His estimate of the price was £347 or $1,735,even then a remarkably modest sum. It went to The Miller Memorial Library, Univ of Wisconsin in 1930. The discounted prices quoted for each of his books are still helpful even today though they must be multiplied by well over 200 to account for inflation. A farm worker in 1930 earned £1.50 a week ; today £320 . His price of 2/6d for a copy Cowan's 'Guide' would equate to more than £6 today. Walker has been quoted frequently,as a perceptive judge,in entries in this catalogue.

60   -   BAB

752   Walker, Lt. Col H J O
Another

814   1929   1985   -   Limp

copy. Reprint   -

15   -   BAB

753   Walker, Lt. Col H J O
Another

814   1929   1985   -   Limp

copy. Reprint.   -

15   -   BAB

754 Warder, J
The True Amazons or the Monarchy of Bees

74	1712	1713	2nd	Browned but sound

Portrait of Warder. Dedicated to Queen Anne.

275	-	ANT

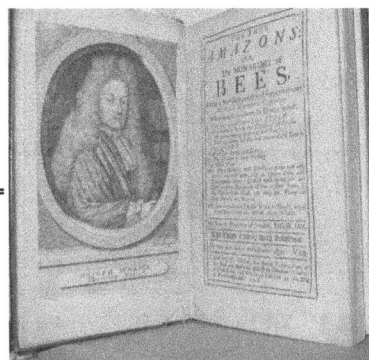

755 Warder, J *Another*

74	1712	1722	5th	Lacks title page. Nice binding

The governance of a QUEEN,breeding,wars,enemies,and how to
handle them in straw hives and transparent boxes for profit Also how
to make mead.. Joseph Warder,physician of Croydon,sold by John
Pemberton at the Buck and Sun over against St Dunstans Church in Fleet Street. Contains a letter answering a charge
by Nourse that Warder had 'largely transcribed from others'.

250	-	ANT

756 Warder, J *Another*

74	1712	1765	9th	Bound with 789 and 714 handsome binding	-

500	-	ANT

757 Warder, J *Another*

74	1712	1712	1st	Coarse cloth. No portrait

"The author of this work has been a Prebyterian,a soldier,a quack and everything…But for bees, I have been
acquainted with some Gentlemen who have had the curiosity to visit his Bee-hives,that no man in the world did
properly understand them better."

250	-	ANT

758 Warder, J *Another*

74	1712	1716	-	Cover loose	-

200	-	ANT

759 Warder, J *Another*

74	1712	1716	3rd	Nice copy -

250	-	ANT

760 Webb, A *Beekeeping for Profit & Pleasure*

817	1945	1947	2nd	(6 copies - 5 with dw)

Illustrations by Davis and Martin-Duncan who wrote the foreword. Encouragement and instruction for novices.
Simple drawings. Originally published in New York, but edited to reflect beekeeping practice in the UK.

7	6	20thC

761 Webster,Walter B *The Book of Bee-keeping*

401	1888	1938	7th	hb

"A bright,well-written little book with good illustrations…repeatedly republished…revised and partly
rewritten"(in1938 and 1947) (Fraser) He was a regular contributor to the BBJ in the early era of bar-framed hives.
He invented a 'fumigator' with a sponge soaked in carbolic acid,creosote and ammonia. It failed! Died 1929.

20	-	OLD

762 **Webster, W B**   *Another*

| 401 | 1888 | - | | No date. Tatty |

18pps of adverts

| 25 | - | OLD | |

---

763 **Webster, W B**   *Another*

| 401 | 1888 | 1901 | 2nd | - | - |

| 30 | - | OLD | |

---

764 **Webster, W B**   *Another*

| 401 | 1888 | early 20th | | Limp cover loose | - |

| 15 | - | OLD | |

---

765 **Webster, W B**   *Another*

| 401 | 1888 | 1908 | 4th | HB. With all faults. | - |

| 5 | - | OLD | |

---

766 **Webster, W B**   *Another*

| 401 | 1888 | 1947 | 8th | Loose cover. Limp | - |

| 5 | - | OLD | |

---

767 **Webster, W B**   *Another*

| 401 | 1888 | 1938 | 7th | Loose cover. Limp | - |

| 5 | - | OLD | |

---

768 **Wedmore, E B**   *The Ventilation of Beehives*

| 821 | 1947 | - | 1st | dw |

A Bee Craft book. A scientific study of a long-standing debating point offering more research information than most beekeepers need to know or can use to advantage.

| 25 | - | 20thC | |

---

769 **Wedmore, E B**   *Another*

| 821 | 1947 | - | 1st | dw mended | - |

| 10 | - | 20thC | |

---

770 **Wedmore, E B**   *Another*

| 821 | 1947 | - | 1st | dw | - |

| 25 | - | 20thC | |

771a **Wedmore, E B**   *A Manual of Beekeeping*

| 818 | 1932 | 1942 | 1st reprint | - |

: for English-speaking beekeepers. He was president of BBKA. A Surrey electrical engineer. Devised divisible frames and a metal indicator for combs.Recognised by Mace as a 'bee-master'. Favours single-walled hives, 'deprecated packing' and advocated good ventilation. 'The best packing for bees is bees'. The manual covers everything the beekeeper needs to know.

| 12 | - | 20thC | |

771b Wedmore, E B   *Another*

818	1932	1946	reprint of 2nd (rev. and corr.)	-		-
12	-	20thC				

reprint of 2nd (rev. and corr.)

818   1932   1946   reprint of 2nd (rev. and corr.)   -   -
12   -   20thC

771c Wedmore, E B   *Another*

818   1932   1947   reprint of 46   -   -
12   -   20thC

771d Wedmore, E B   *Another*

818   1932   1979   reprint of 2nd   -
last reprint of 2nd by BBNO
12   -   20thC

772 Wedmore, E B   *Successful Beekeeping*

820   1946   -   1st   Spine half bare   -
4   -   20thC

773 Wedmore, E B   *Another*

820   1946   -   1st   -
10   -   20thC

774 Wedmore, E B   *Another*

820   1946   -   1st   Chipped dw   -
8   -   20thC

775 Wedmore, E B   *Another*

820   1946   -   1st   (2 copies) -
8   2   20thC

776 Weekly Memorials for the Ingenious   *12 issues*

-    1681   -   -   Nicely rebound
Digests of books. P 2 refers to black Abyssinian bees with no sting. P 27 Bees generated without copulation from the dung of horses or oxen.
100   -   ANT

777 Weightman, C   *The Border Bees*

822   1961   -   1st   dw. (2 copies).
:anecdotes and memoirs of twenty years 1940-60. Consett, Co. Durham. His chapter 10 'People' characterises 15 famous beekeepers of his acquaintance.
15   2   20thC

778 Weiss, Edward A   *The Queen & I*

-    1978   -   1st   dw. Mint.
Step-by-step instruction for the beginning beekeeper. An engaging, friendly style
12   -   USA

779 **Wells, G**   *The Two Queen System of Queen Rearing*
411   1894   1894   1st   short guide pamphlet – well used
A controversial system, following Virgil and Bromwich in using two queens in boxes separated by a division board, fiercely argued in the BBJ in the late 1890's and ultimately abandoned -except by Ron Brown.
20   -   OLD

780 **Whiston, J** *History of Staffs BKA*
824   1976   -   1st   Paperback-
8   -   MOD

781 **Whitcombe & Douglas**   *Bees Are My Business*
825 J395 1956 1955   -   1st   -   Autobiographical account of commercial beekeeping in the USA.
Excellent family photographs. Pub. Gollancz.
15   -   20thC

782 **White, C N**   *Pleasurable Beekeeping*
414   1895   1895   1st   Spine weak.
Adverts for Blow, books and chicken food. BBKA fin de siecle lecturer for County Councils under Technical Education Schemes to help cottagers.
40   -   OLD

783 **White, C N**   *Another*
414   1895   1895   1st   -   -
40   -   OLD

784 **White, C N**   *Bees, A Practical handbook*
448   1909   1909   1st   -
Vinton's Country Series. Adverts for 83 books on agriculture and sporting subjects.
20   -   OLD

785 **Whitehead, Dr S B**   *Bees to the Heather*
828   1954   1954   1st   -
Pub. Faber. With a letter from the BBC about a review to be broadcast. All about heather honey and where to harvest it in the UK.
30   -   20thC

786 **Whitehead, Dr. S B**   *Honeybees & their Management*
827   1946   -   1st   (3 copies)
In two parts. The first is the lifecycle of the bee and how to manage it. The second deals with more advanced techniques, including a bibliography of preferred books.'The amateur needs instruction.... and few give it as clearly and sensibly as Dr. Whitehead.' (New Statesman).
10   3   20thC

787 Whitehead, S   *Another*

| 827 | 1946 | 1949 | 2nd & 3rd (2 copies) - |
| 8 | 2 | 20thC | |

---

788 Wildman, Daniel
A Complete Guide to the Management of Bees throughout the Year

| 125 | 1773 | 1801 | 15th |

Bound in with Cotton's Short and Simple letter to Cottagers (See 132) [2nd Ed 1838 Cost 6 pence -Gentlemen,2 pence -cottagers. One of 20 editions to 1819.] The first American book by A Farmer of Massachusetts of 1729 was taken from D Wildman

| 300 | - | ANT |

---

789 Wildman, Daniel   *An inquiry into bees*

| 125 | 1773 | 1774 | 4th | Bound in with 756 and 714. Price as for 756 |

Daniiel was the nephew of Thomas. He used red cedar in his appliance business.

| 0 | - | ANT |

---

790 Wildman, Thomas   *A Treatise on the Management of Bees*

| 119 | 1768 | - | 1st | Back cover detached and some spine damage o/w very clean copy |

their natural history and cultivation together with wasps and hornets.Thomas left Plymouth for London in. 1766. His patron was George III and his book dedicated to the Queen for which he won a noble subscription list ,(in the text). He was a clever performer of beekeeping trick shows as was his nephew Daniel. He favoured piling up flat-topped skeps.. "His treatise shows culture and an unusual knowledge of continental beekeeping" (IBRA) 3 large plates.

| 400 | - | ANT |

---

791 Wildman, Thomas   *Another*

| 119 | 1768 | - | 1st | Complete and v clean | - |
| 450 | - | ANT |

---

792 Wildman, Thomas   *Another*

| 119 | 1768 | - | 1st | Cover loose | - |
| 400 | - | ANT |

---

793 Wildman, Thomas   *Another*

| 119 | 1769 | 1770 | 2nd | Reound. Lacks 3 plates   no Appendix. | - |
| 300 | - | ANT |

---

794 Wildman, Thomas   *Another*

| 119 | 1769 | 1770 | 2nd | Lacks 3 plates. Uncut. Has an Appdx 'De Re Rustica' |
| 400 | - | ANT |

---

795 Wildman, Thomas   *Another*

| 119 | 1769 | 1970 | - | Reprint of 2nd edition |

Kingsmead

| 10 | - | ANT |

796   Wildman, Thomas   *Another*

| 119 | 1769 | 1970 | - | Mint. Reprint of 1770 edition. dw |
| 10 | - | ANT | | |

---

797   Williams, Canning   *The Story of the Hive*

| 829 | 1928 | - | 1st | (3 copies) |

: a bee-lover's book. Pub. Black. 'Something that will uplift and satisfy the mind and soul….the study of the honeybee'. Intended for the general reader rather than the apiarist.

| 6 | 3 | 20thC | | |

---

798   Williams, Kit   *Mystery Book*

| - | 1970's? | - | 1st | Puzzle book |

Searching for hidden treasure. A work of art. Lyrical and poetic.

| 15 | - | MOD | | |

---

799   Williams, Kit   *Another*

| - | 1970's? | - | 1st | Puzzle book | - |
| 15 | - | MOD | | | |

---

800   Winter, T S   *Queen Rearing*

| - | 1980's | - | - | |

New Zealand booklet. 26 pps. About grafting into cell cups.

| 5 | - | MOD | | |

---

801   Wittish, Boris   *A Taste of Honey*

| - | 1978 | 1981 | 1st UK | From German |

Not by Shiela Delaney! 80 pps of recipes

| 12 | - | MOD | | |

---

802   Wood, Rev John   *Half Hours with a Naturalist*

| 384 | 1885 | 1885 | 1st |

Yet another man of the cloth with time to entertain himself with bees. A popular lecturer and writer on natural history and scientific matters. Very good large illustrations showing skeps and swarms. Bees in pps 204-234

| 40 | - | OLD | |

---

803   Wood, Rev John   *Bees; Their Habits*

| 278 | 1853 | 1872 | - | Orange cloth bound |

:their habits,management and treatment. 16 pps of adverts for books.

| 35 | - | OLD | | |

---

804   Wood, Rev John   *Another*

| 278 | 1853 | - | - | Grey cloth with 1884 advert for drugs etc. Cover shaky. | - |
| 30 | - | OLD | | | |

805   Wood, Rev John   *Another*

278   1853   new ed   New ed. London. Purple cloth bound, contains advert from 1884

There were many editions with varying illustrations and covers but similar text.'A well-judged compilation' (Fraser)

30   -   OLD

---

806   Worlidge, John
***Systema Agriculturae, or the mystery of
husbandry discovered***

43   1669   1675   2nd   -

"A distinguished writer on agricultural matters. Worlidge was a
practical bee-master and made many experiments.(Walker) Bees
pps168-188. He had a poor opinion of Gedde's wooden cases
and glass windows.

400   -   ANT

**807   Worlidge,John   *The Mystery of
Husbandry and Kalendarium Rusticum***

43   1669   -

GM Trevelyan,in his 'Social History' says this was the first
attempt to advise on agricultural matters on a large scale. In the
explanatory dedication opposite the frontispiece is the couplet:
"On the other side hard by the house you see / Th' Apiary for
the industrious Bee"   This book helped point the way to the
'Agricultural Revolution' of the 18th Century.

600   -   ANT

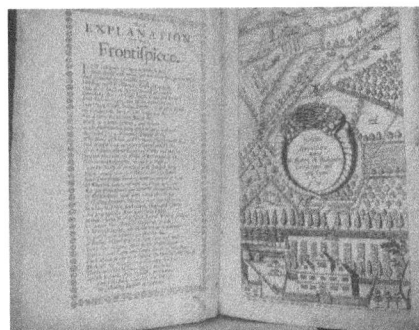

808   Worlidge,John   *Vinetum Britannicum*

54   1678   -

A treatise of cider and other wines.. to which is added a discourse teaching the best way of improving bees. This has
its own title -'Apiarum'. He proposed square boxes in a pile protected in a bee-house.

400   -   ANT

---

809   Yates, J & B   *Beekeeping Study Notes*

-           -   -   -   -

Part of a modern series. A crammer for those studying for BBKA exams.

8   -   MISC

---

810   X   *Various Papers*

20   Various   -   -   -

2 pps of cuts(old),2 mags from Aust & NZ,Prospectus for Sparsholt,6 learned papers by Butler,Free,Paton,Williams,Si
mpson and Scott, pps from New Scientist.

12   -   20thC

---

811   X   *Various catalogues*

-	-	1962 to 1984	-	13 items sold as one Lees, Thornes etc.
5	-	MOD		

812 X *Burtt's Catalogues*

-	1940	-	-	-	-
5	-	MOD			

DESIDERATA

Digby, Sir Kenelm   *The Closet of the eminently learned Sir K D.*
42   -   1669   -   -
About mead and other honey-based drinks. A closet was a small private room used for domestic purposes, including reading.

Dyer, W   *The Apiary laid open*
137   -   1781   -   -
Collaterals again "Retrocoupling bee boxes". Impossibly rare book. -

Dzierzon,   **Dr. J**   *Rational Beekeeping*
365   -   1882   -   -   Dicoverer of parthenogenesis in bees. Edited by Abbott   -   -

Edwardes,Rev T   *Bees as Rent Payers*
430   -   1906   -   -   A plain practical guide for cottagers

Fitzherbert, John   *Book of Husbandry*
1   -   1523   -   -
The first two pages written by an English man on the subject of beekeeping -   -

Hartlib, Samuel   *The Reformed Commonwealth of Bees*
33   -   1655   -   -   A friend of Milton. Describes the octagonal 3-storied hive,with a drawing by Christopher Wren. It was designed by Rev Mew and one such was admired by both Wren and Evelyn. It is the same model that Gedde patented in 1675 and probably influenced Kerr's popular Stewarton hive.Wren's drawing is found in Fraser's 'History'.

Levett, John   *The Ordering of Bees*
24   -   1634   -   -
set forth in a dialogue- about Heresbach,as translated by Googe, and Southerne.   -

Mather, Wiliam   *The young man's companion*
56   -   1681   -   -
A schoolmaster's manual for youth   -

Maxwell, Robert   *The practical beemaster.*
102   -   1747   -   -
"An important work by a well-educated but retrograde beekeeper" (Walker)

Milton, John   *The practical beekeeper*

248   -   1843   -   -

A honey and hive dealer. He used notes left for him by Cotton when he went to N. Zealand. A row ensued and the notes vanished from the 1851 edition.   -

-          -   -

Milton, John   *The London Apiarian Guide*

195   -   1823   -   -

Promotes the newly invented double-topped straw hive.   -

          -          -

Mouffet, Thomas *The theater of insects*

25   -   1634   -   -

Probably the father of Little Miss Muffet. He was an authority on spiders.

-          -   -   -

Munn, Wm A   *A Description of the bar-and-frame hive invented by WA Munn*

250   -   1844   -   -

"Munn's hive ...was regarded by some...as having anticipated the idea of Langstroth and used in litigation in the attempt to invalidate his patent" (Walker) -

          -          -   -

Purchas,Rev Samuel   *A theatre of politicall flying-insects*

35   -   1657   -   -

Concerns 'the right ordering of the bee..' with theological and moral observations and meditations on that subject.

-          -   -   -

Remnant, Richard   *A Discourse or Historie of Bees*

26   -   1637   -   -

He knew workers were female   -

          -          -   -

Roel (Robert Russell)   *Extracts from Huber*

192   -   1822   -   -

A typographical curiosity.Russell cut the type himself and printed the book when he was only 15.

-          -

Southerne,Edmund   *A treatise concerning the right use and ordering of bees.*

12   -   1593   -   -

The first book totally on the subject of bees. It has the famous story about tithes picked up by Cotton

-          -   -   -

Wheler, Sir George   *A journey into Greece*

57   -   1682   -   -

Greek skeps with movable bars recorded, probably for the very first time in Europe. The advantage of being able to inspect frames was ignored for over 150 years.

-      -   -   -

White, Rev Stephen   *Collateral bee-boxes*

109   -   1756   -   -

Suffolk Parson who invented a system adopted and claimed by Nutt in 1832

-      -   -   -

Geoffrey Lawes

Notes

Notes

Geoffrey Lawes

Notes